Mind the blackhole

by Luna Sees

Mind the blackhole

ISBN: 978-1-312-67440-0

Any reference to historical events, real people, or real places are used fictitiously. Names, charactors, and places are products of the authors imagination.

Front cover image by Luna Sees
Book design by Luna Sees

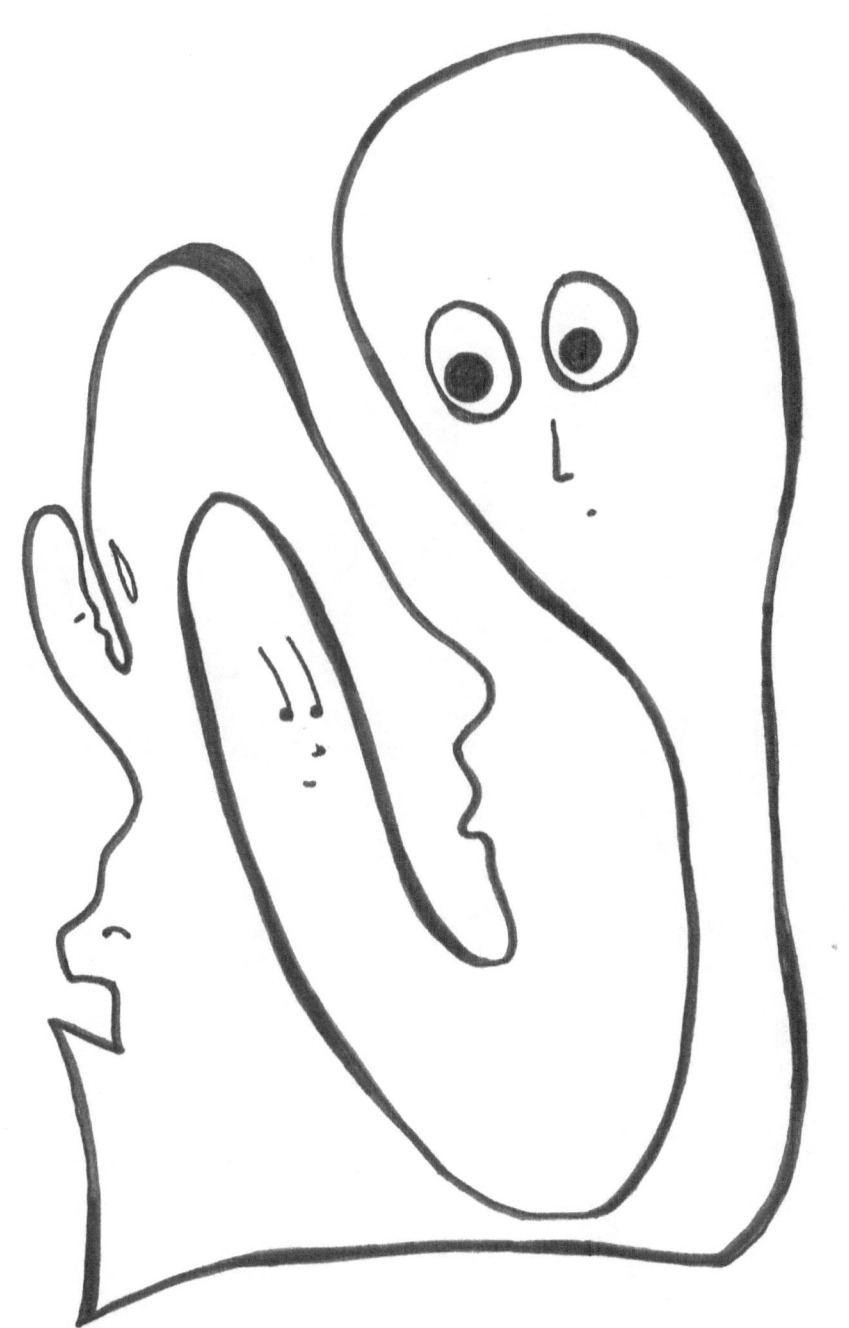

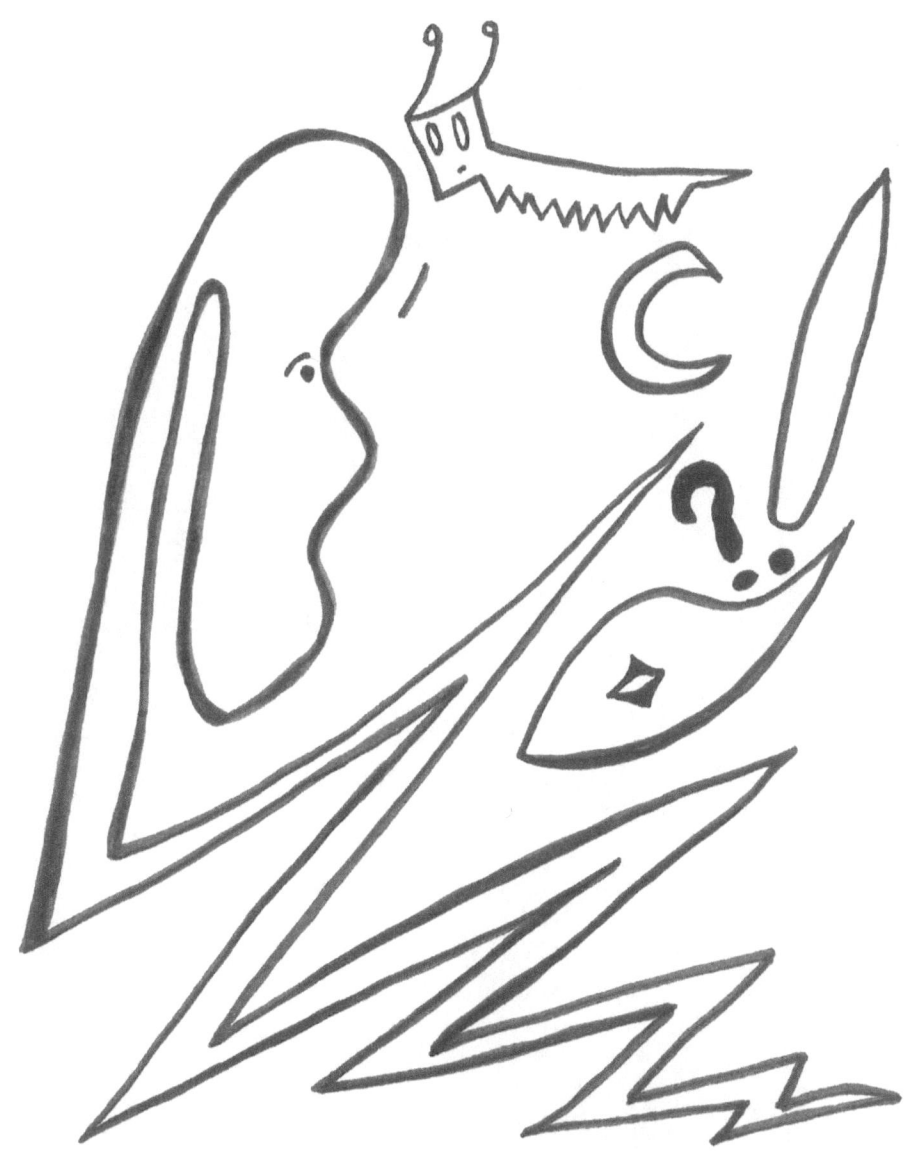

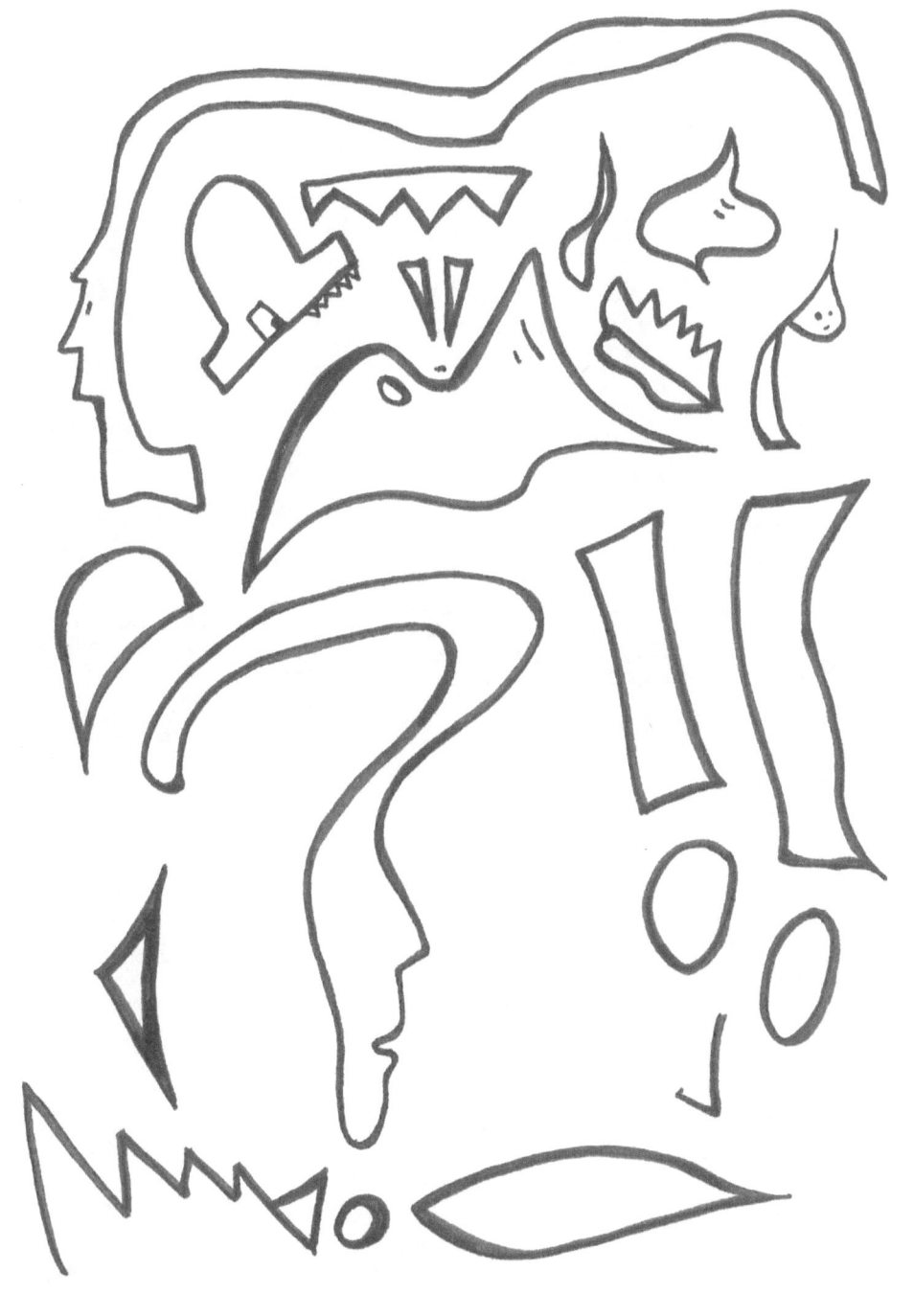

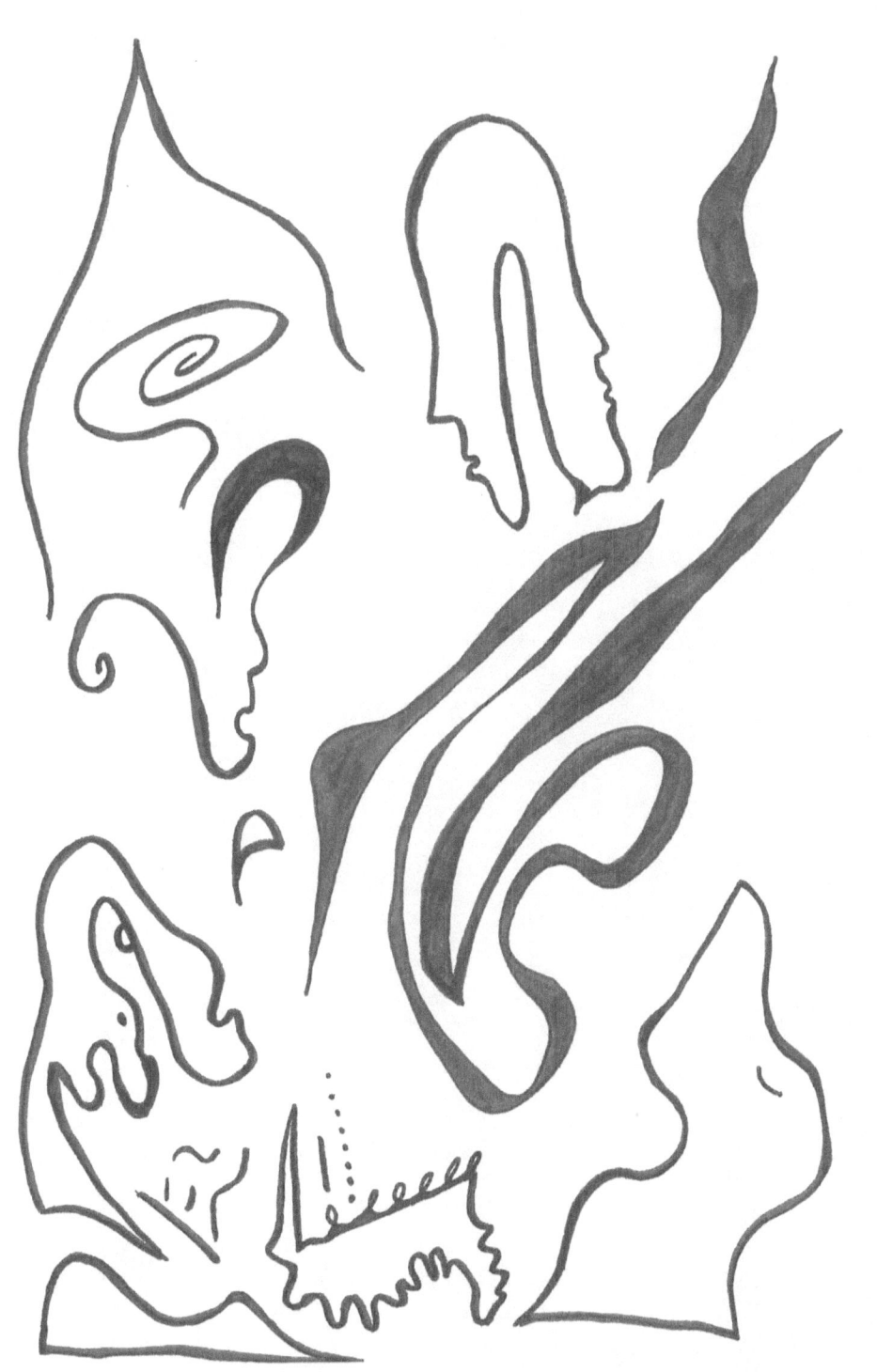

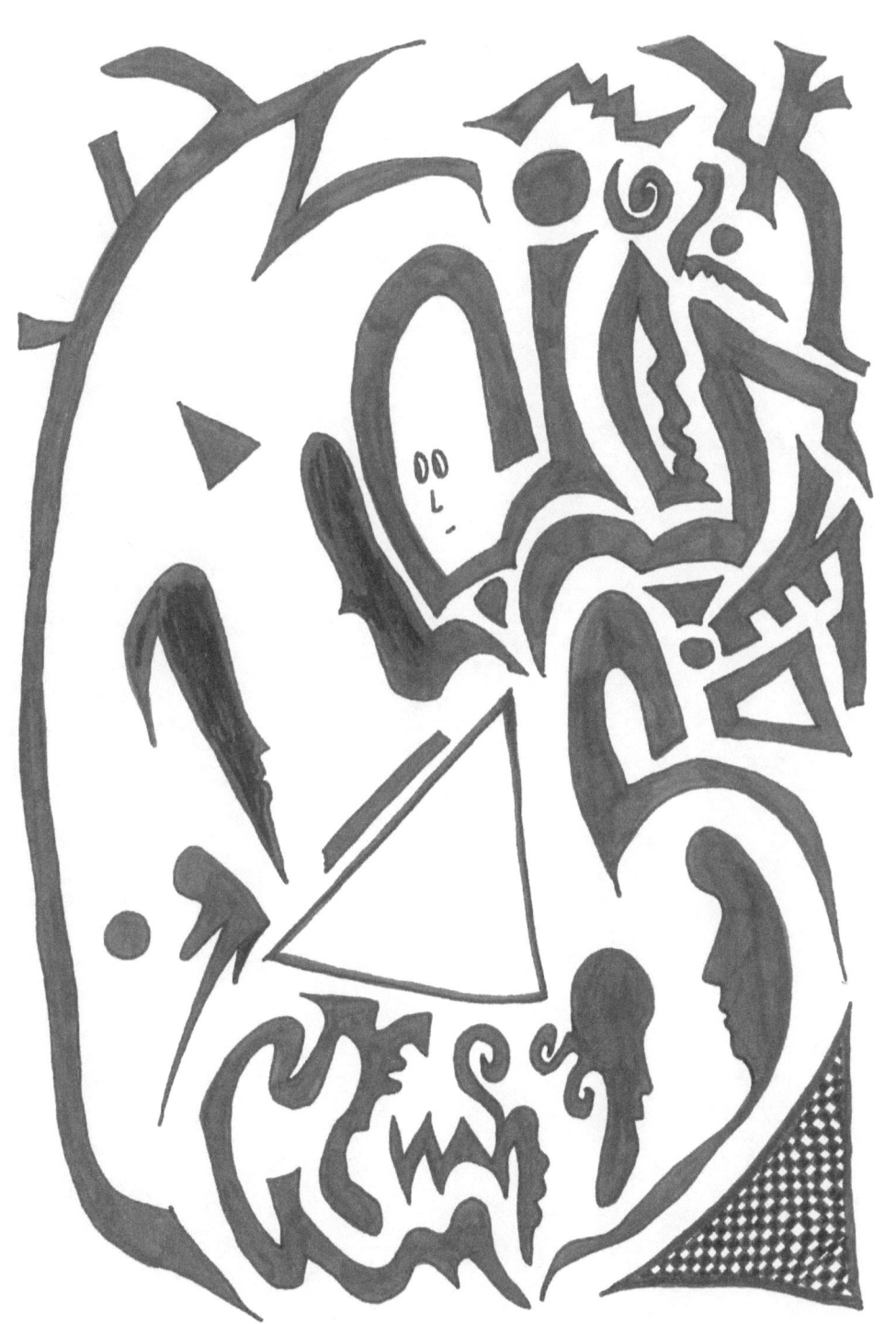

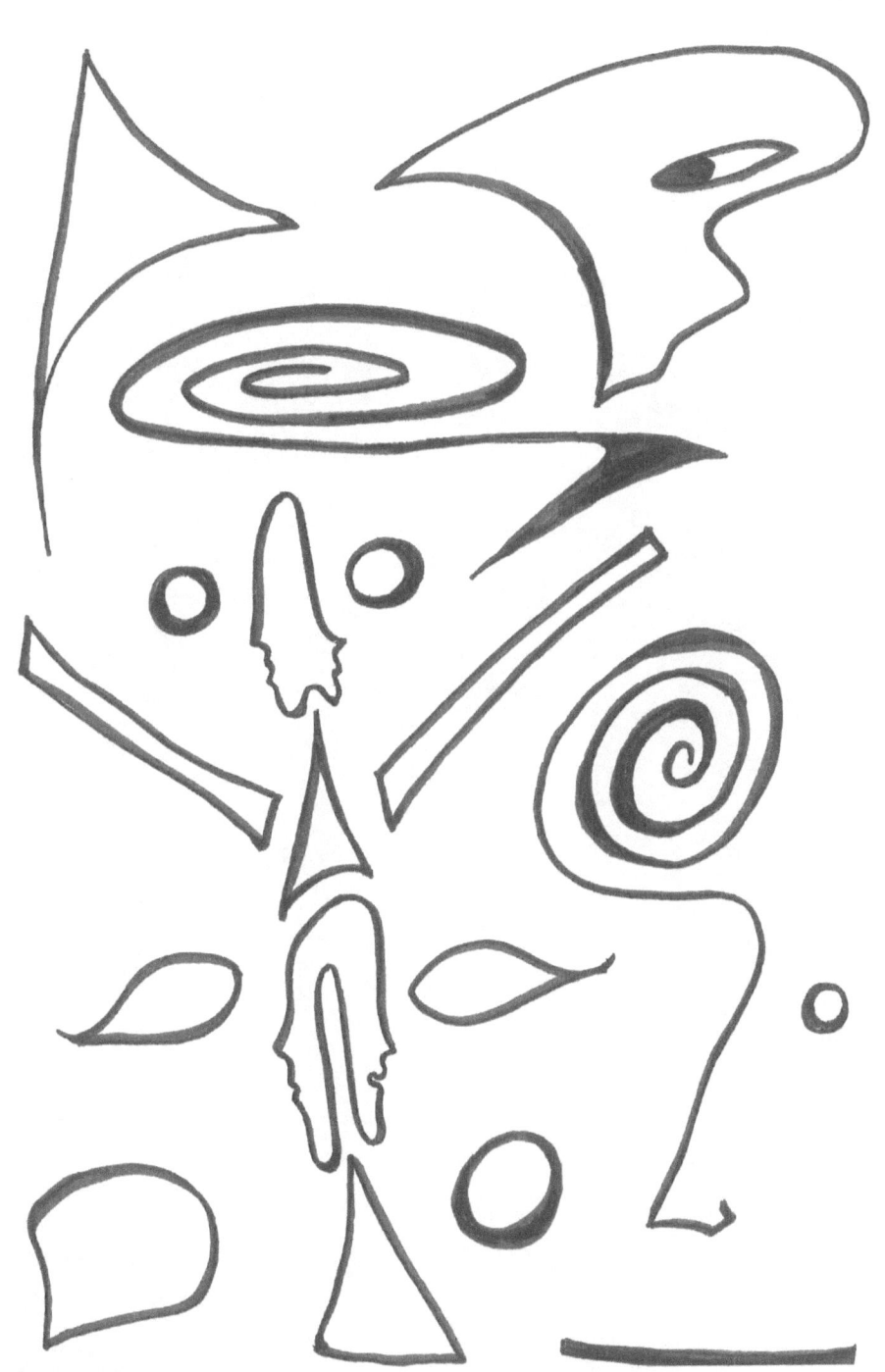

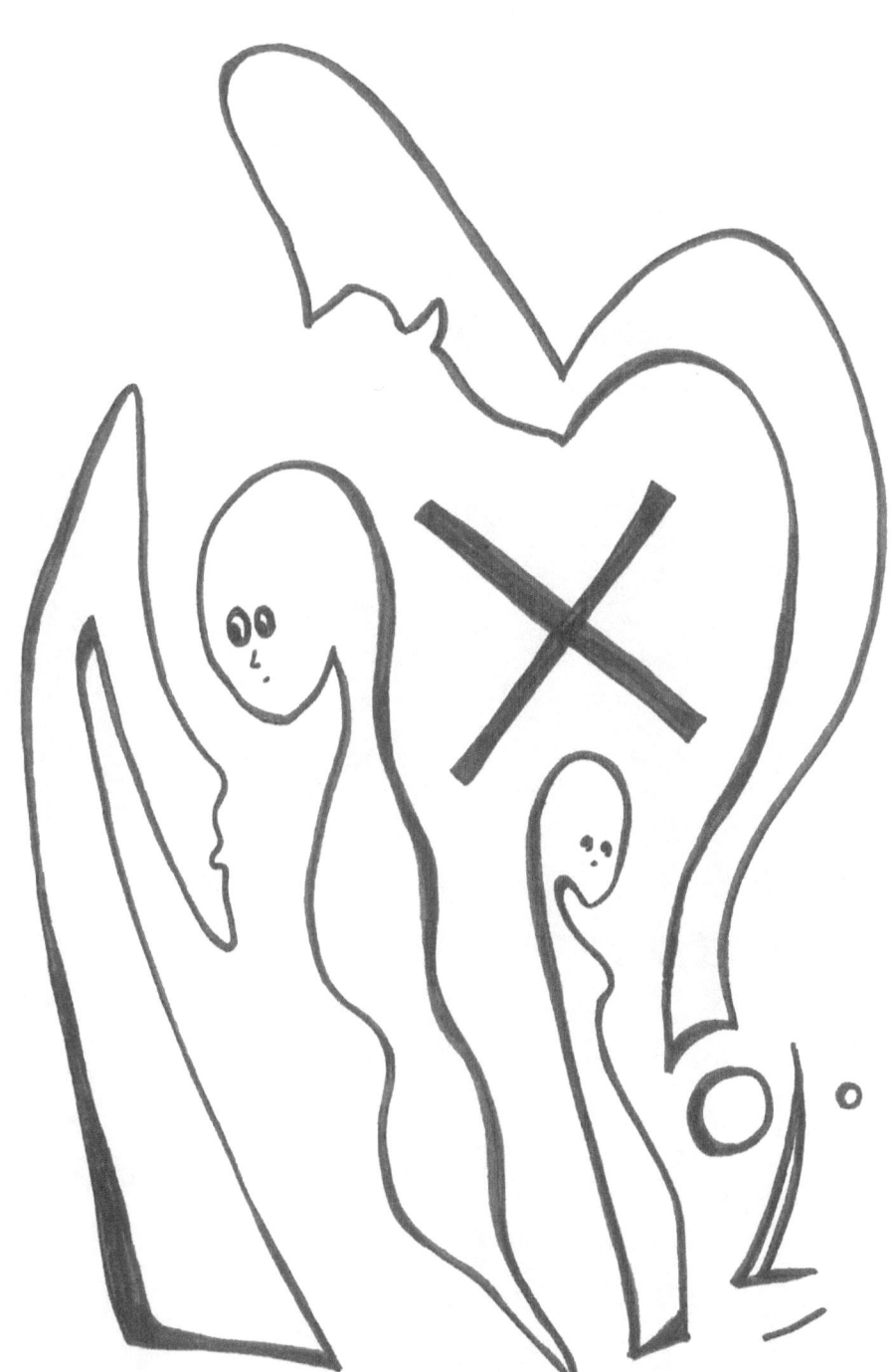

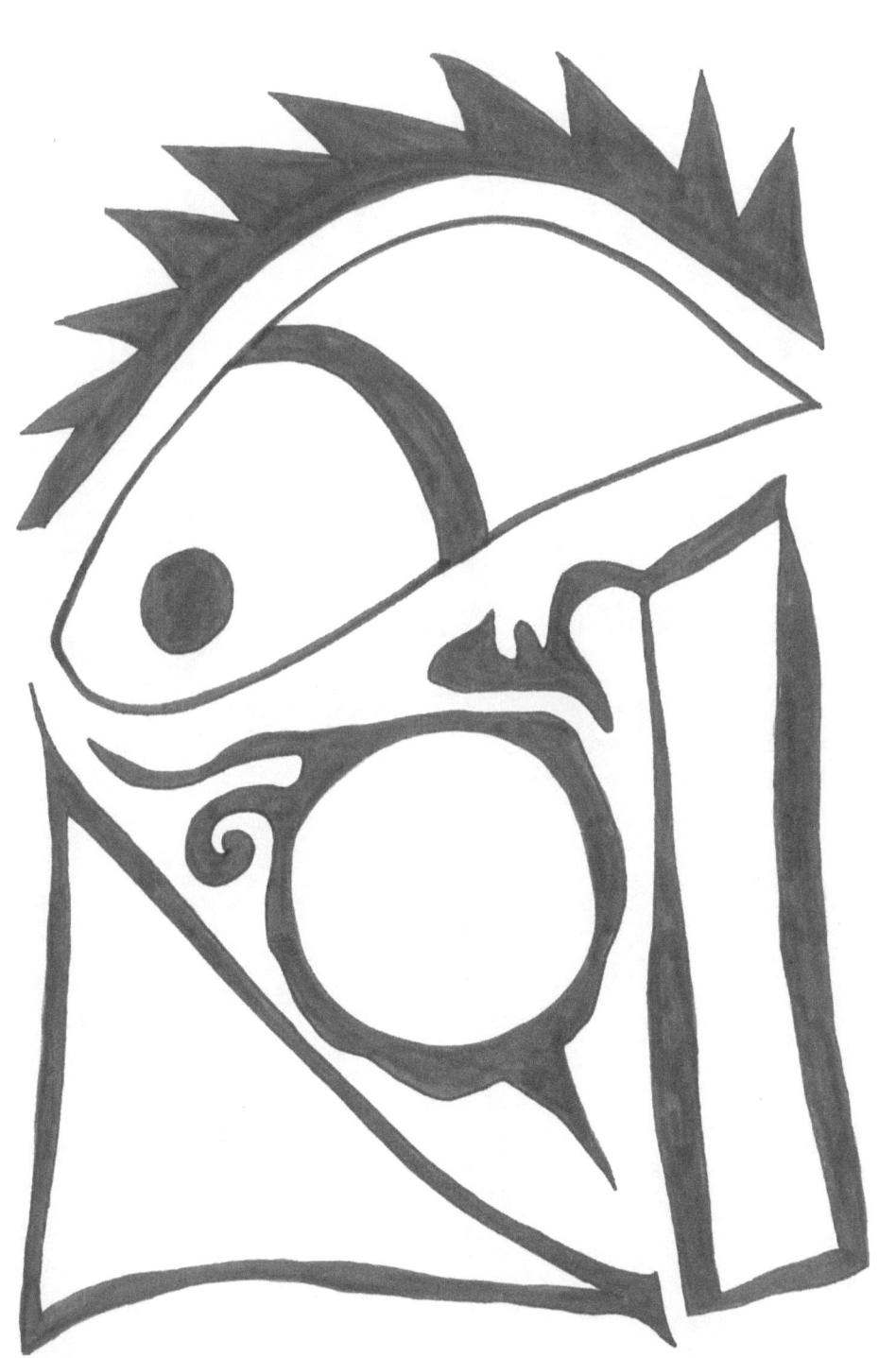

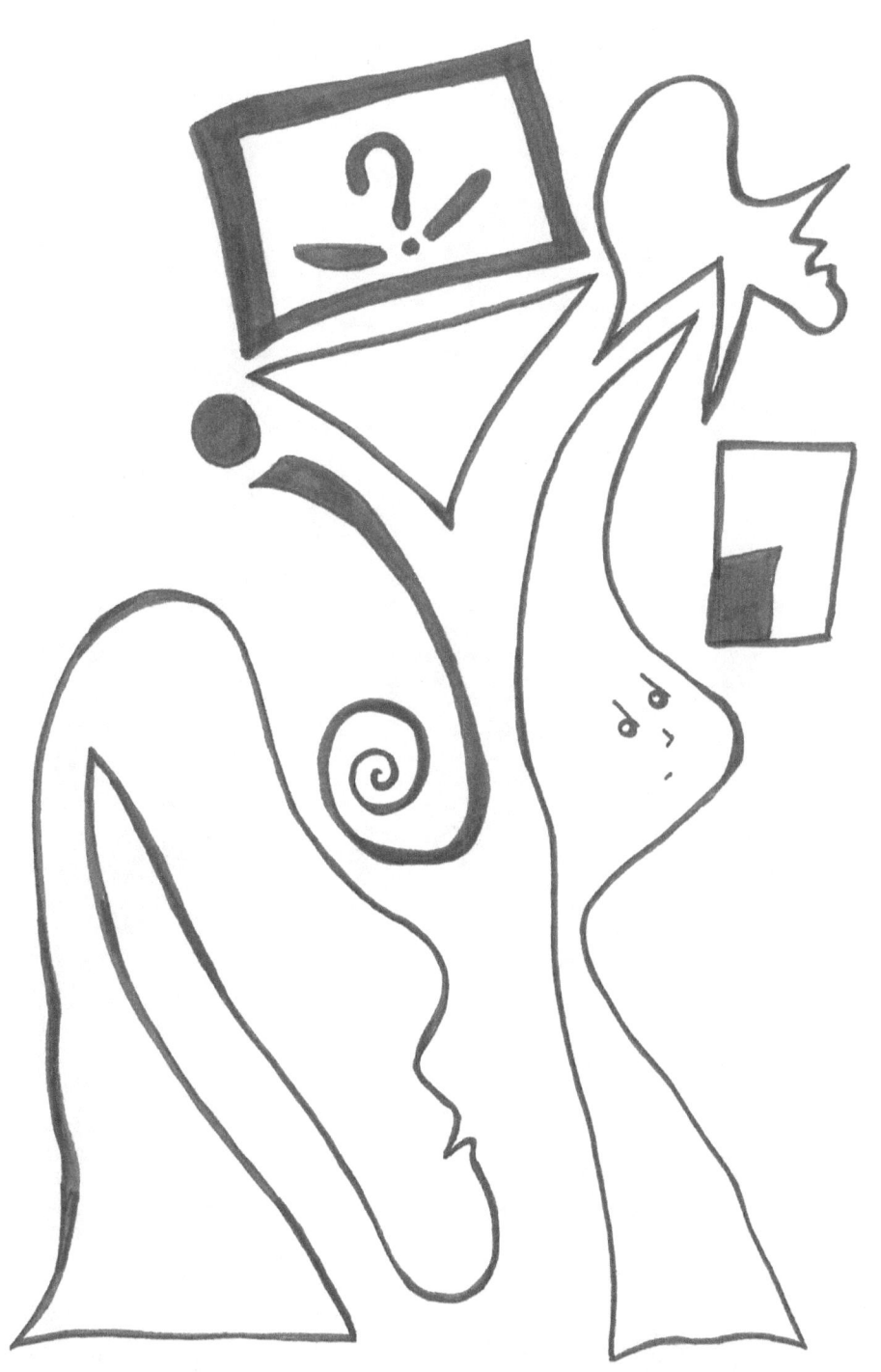

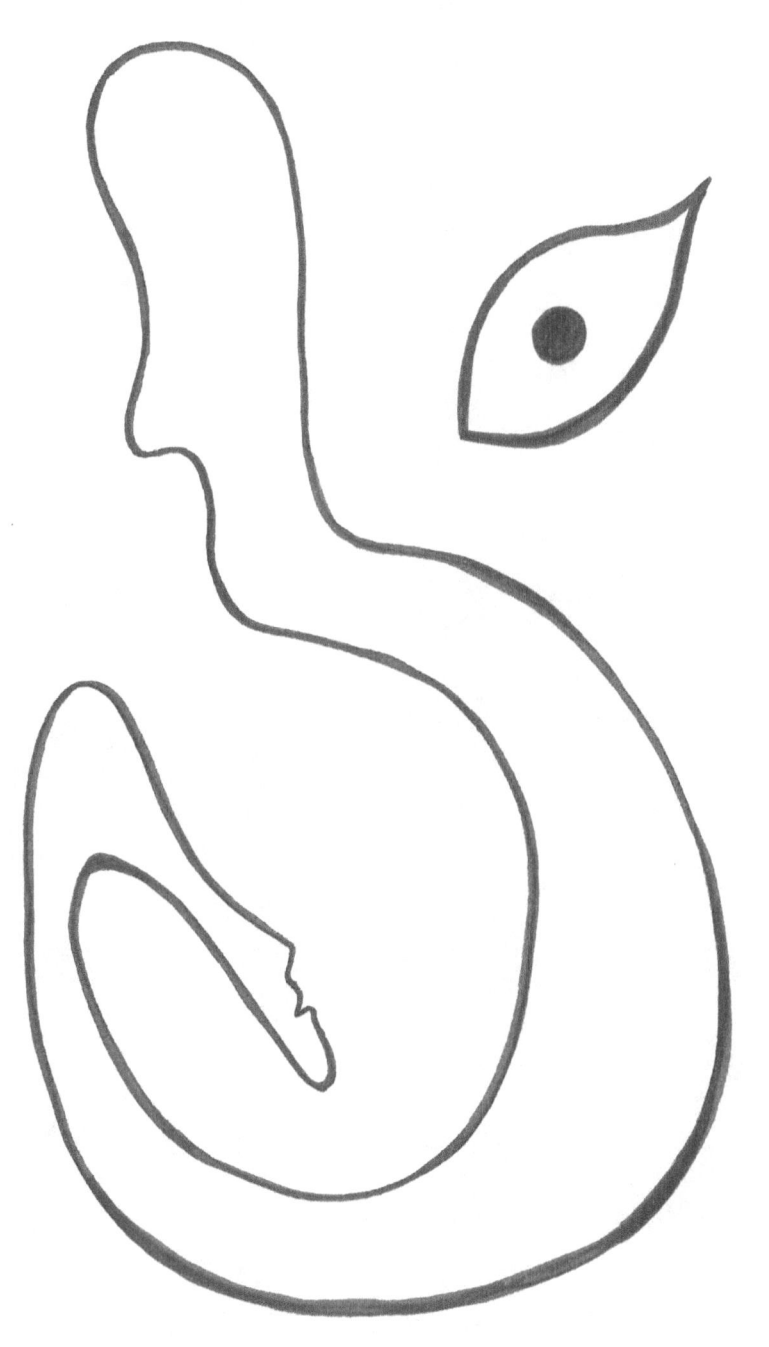

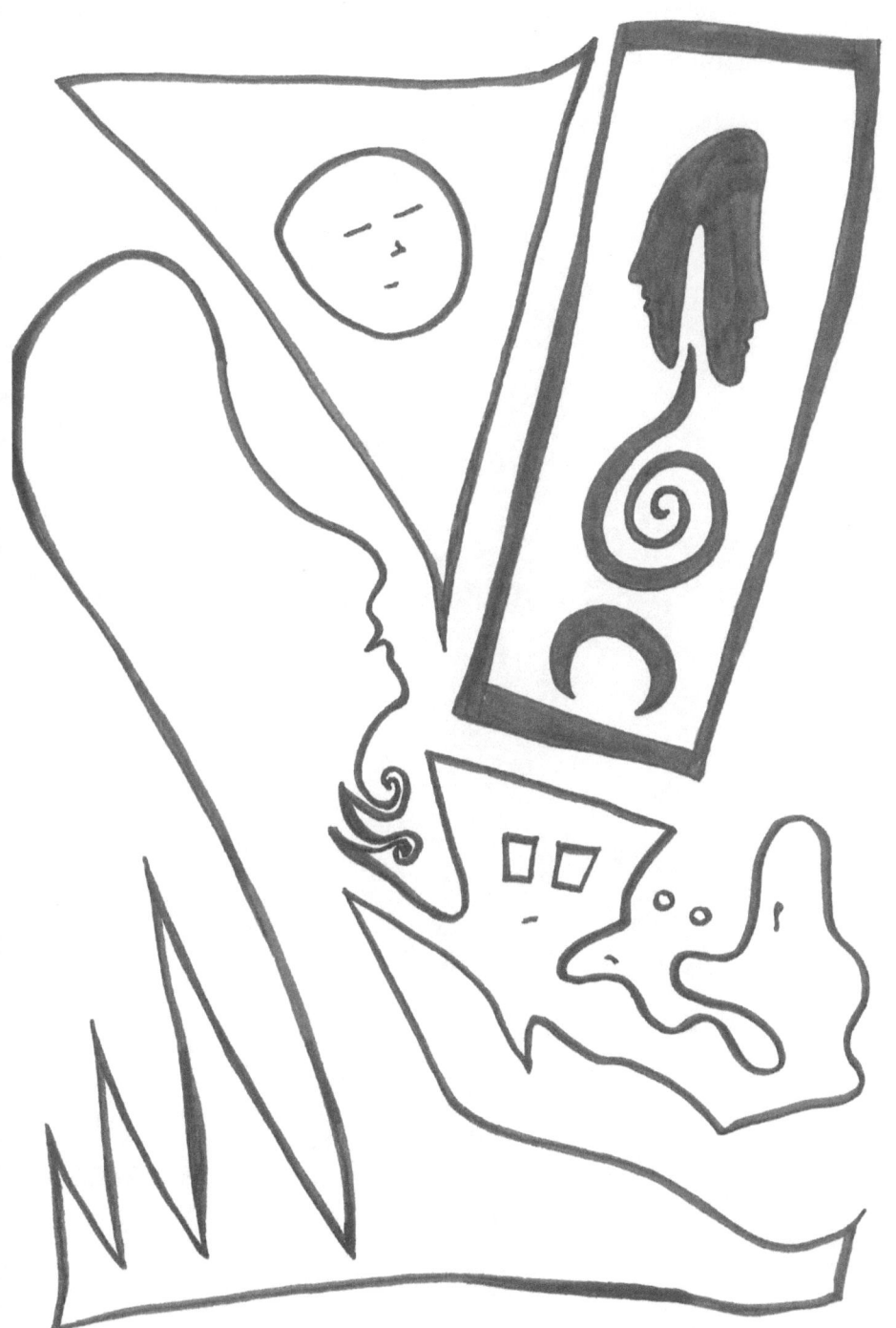

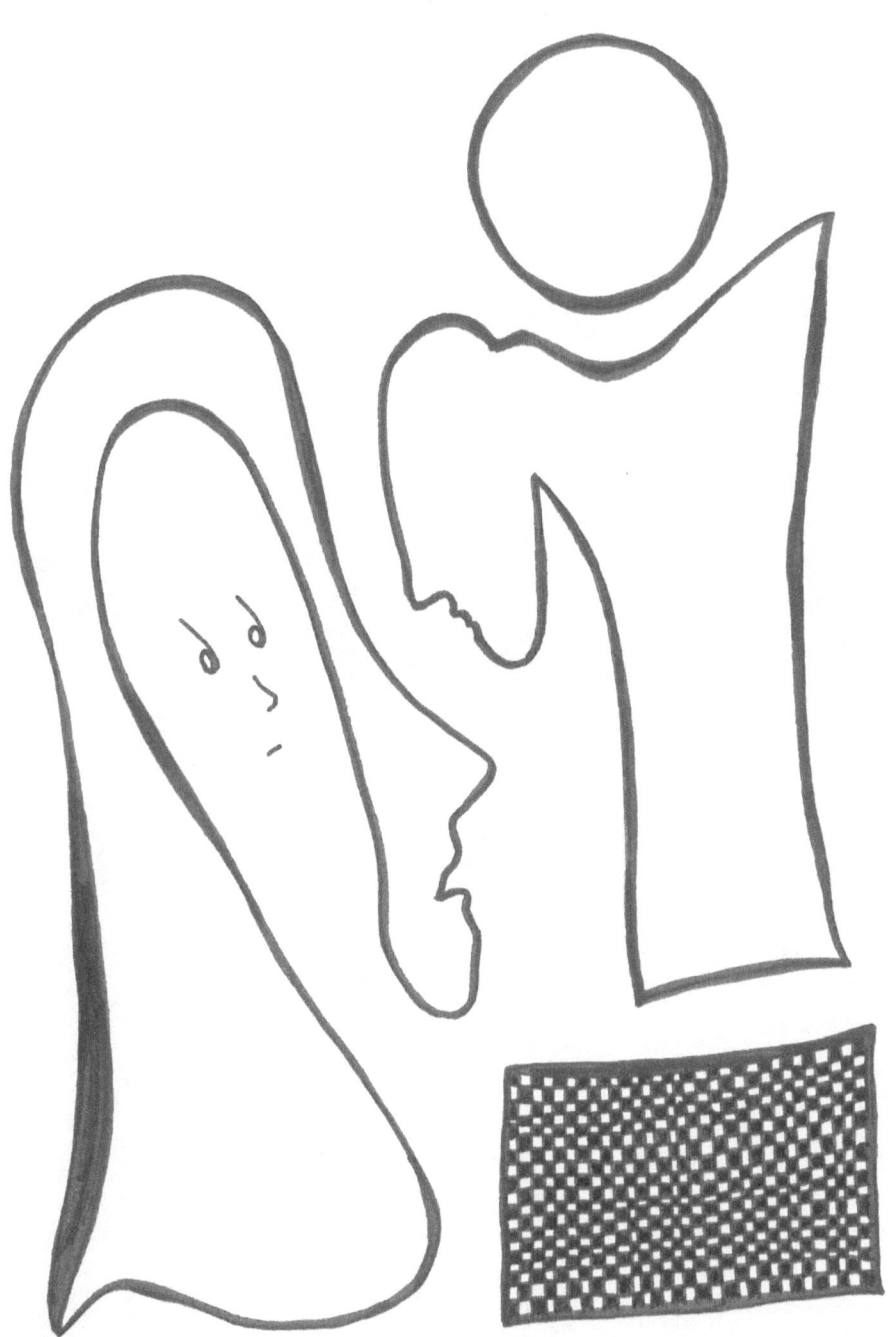

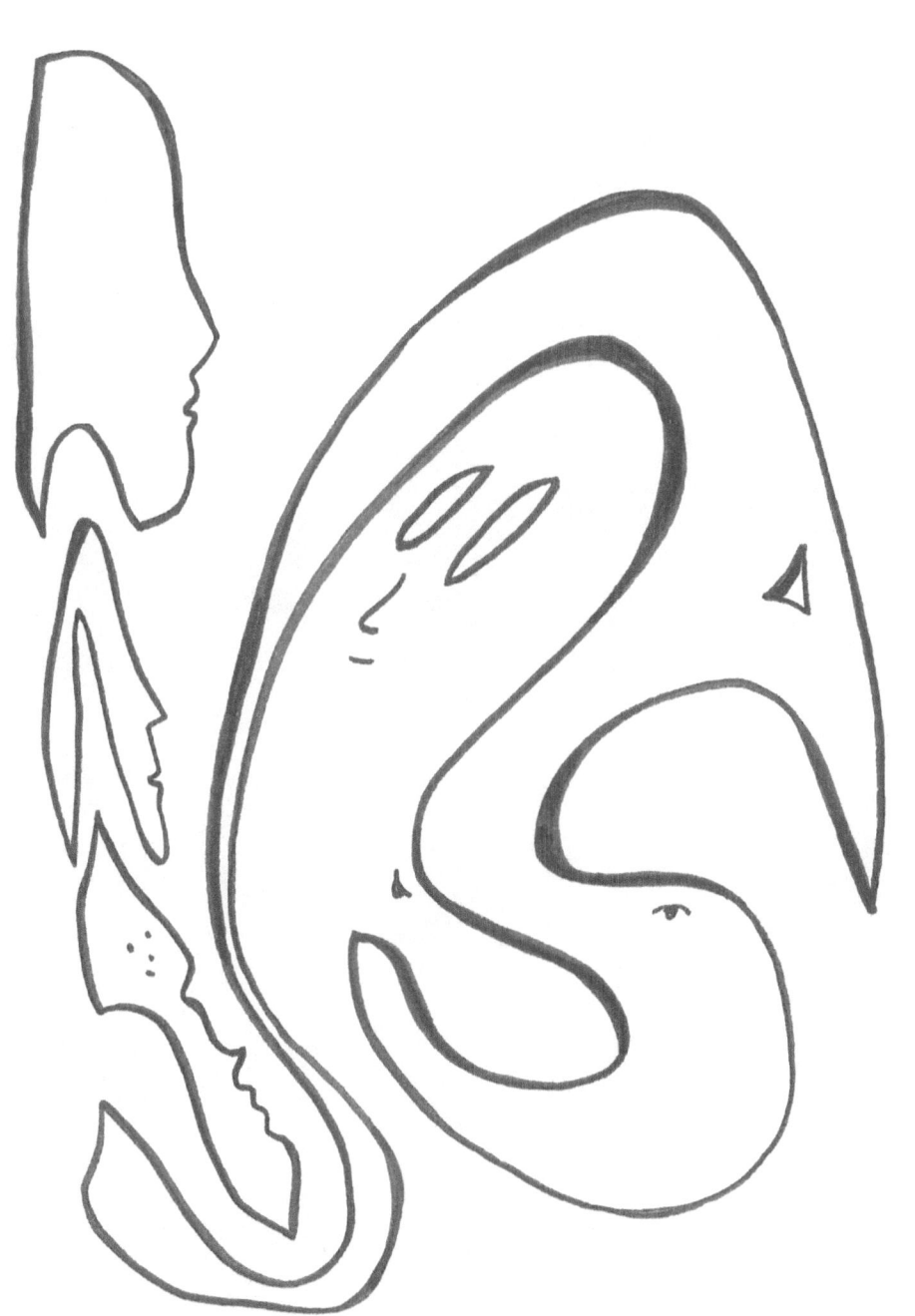

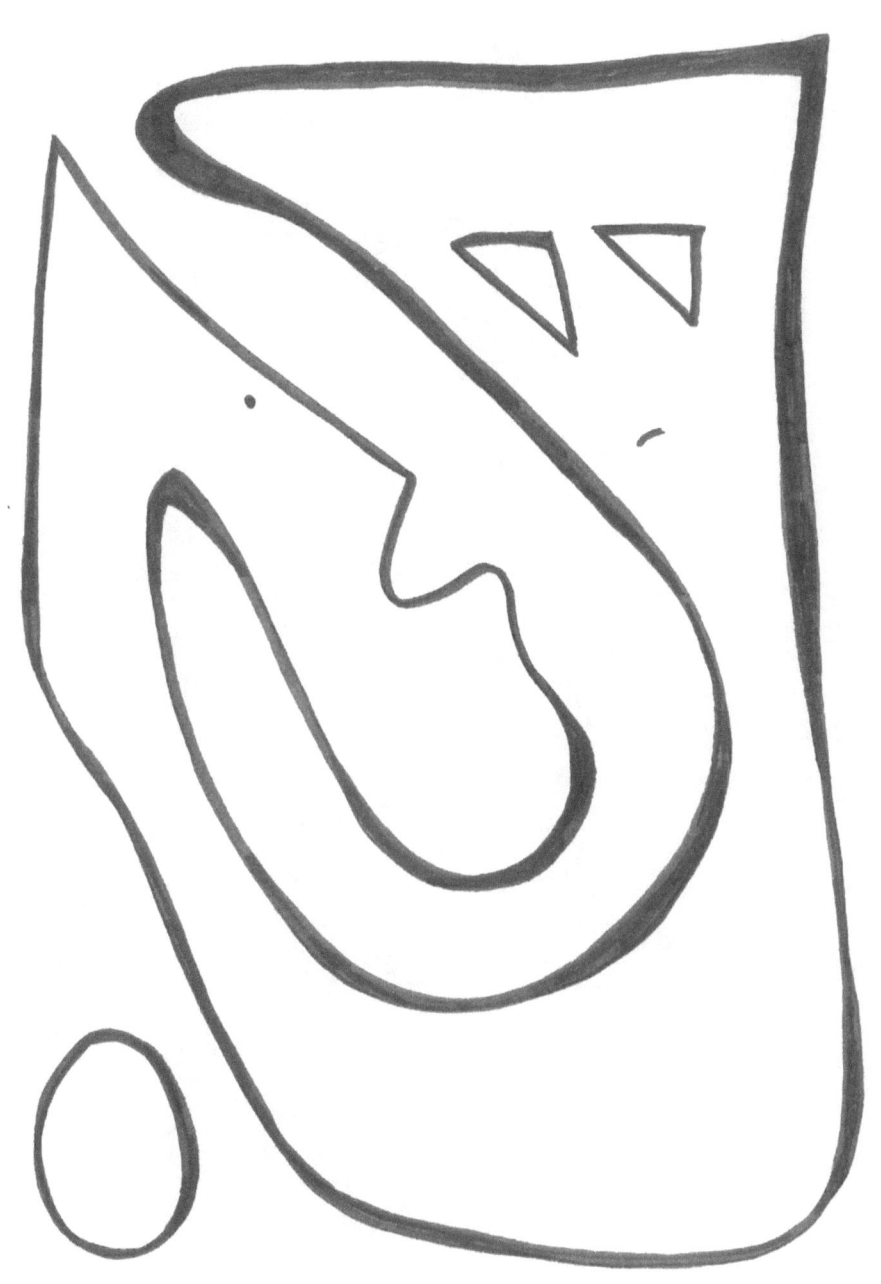

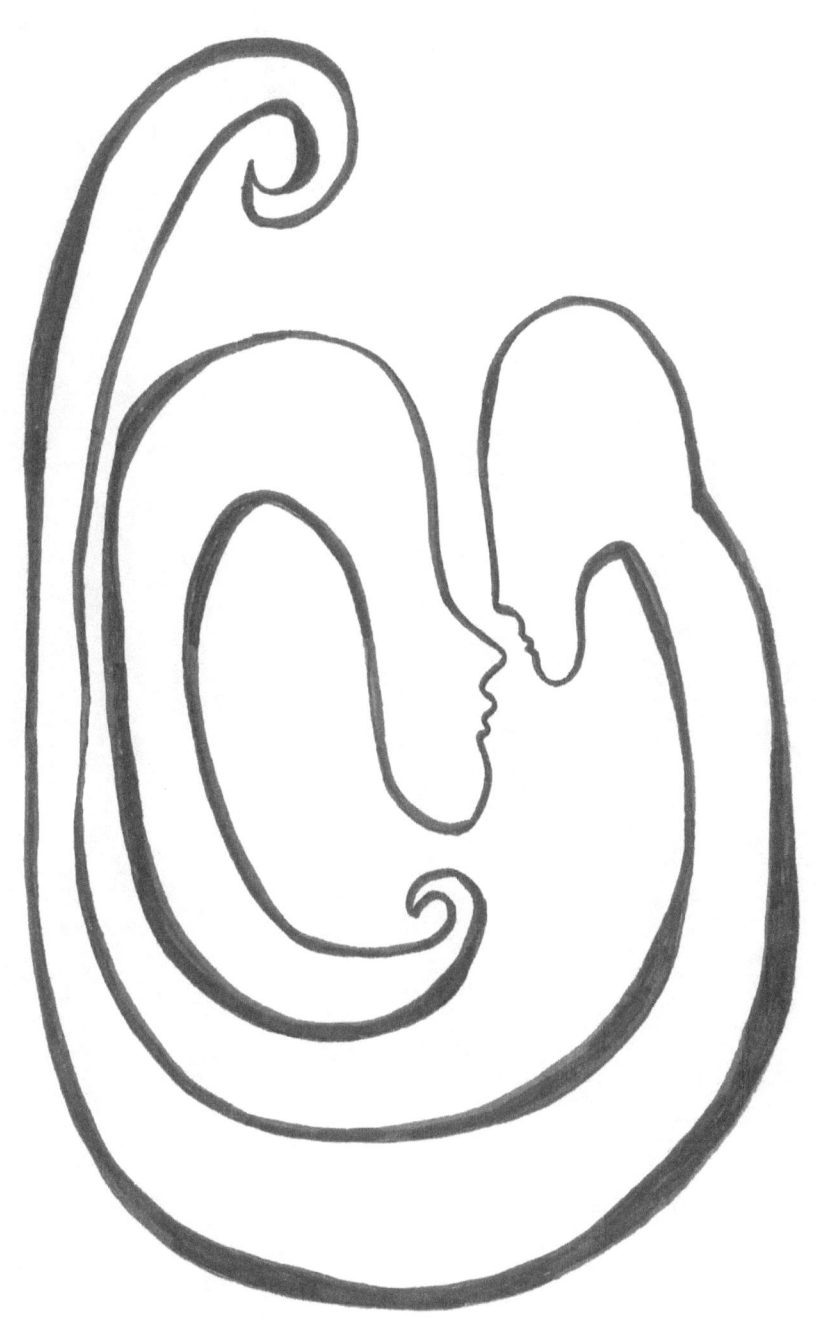

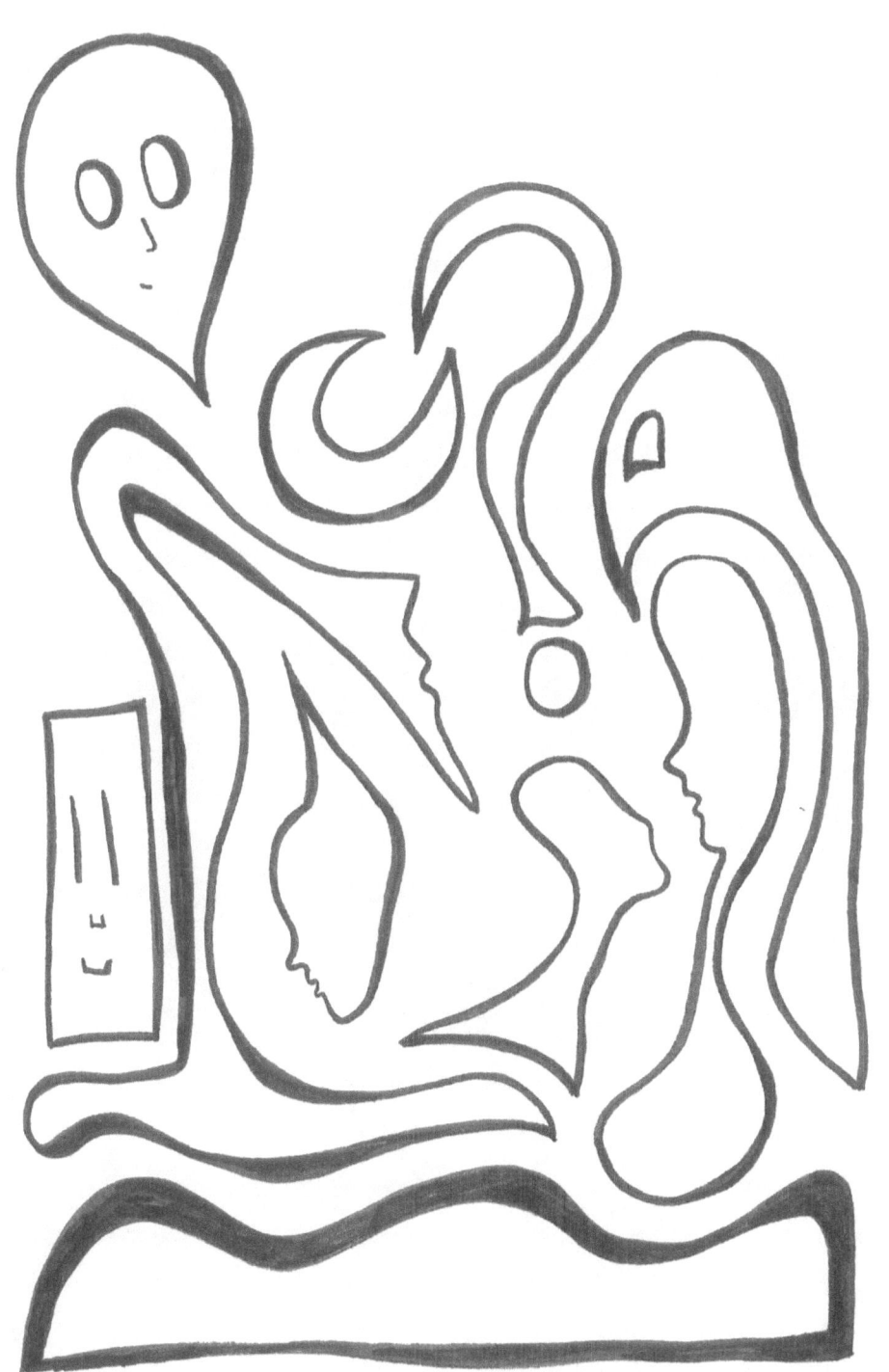

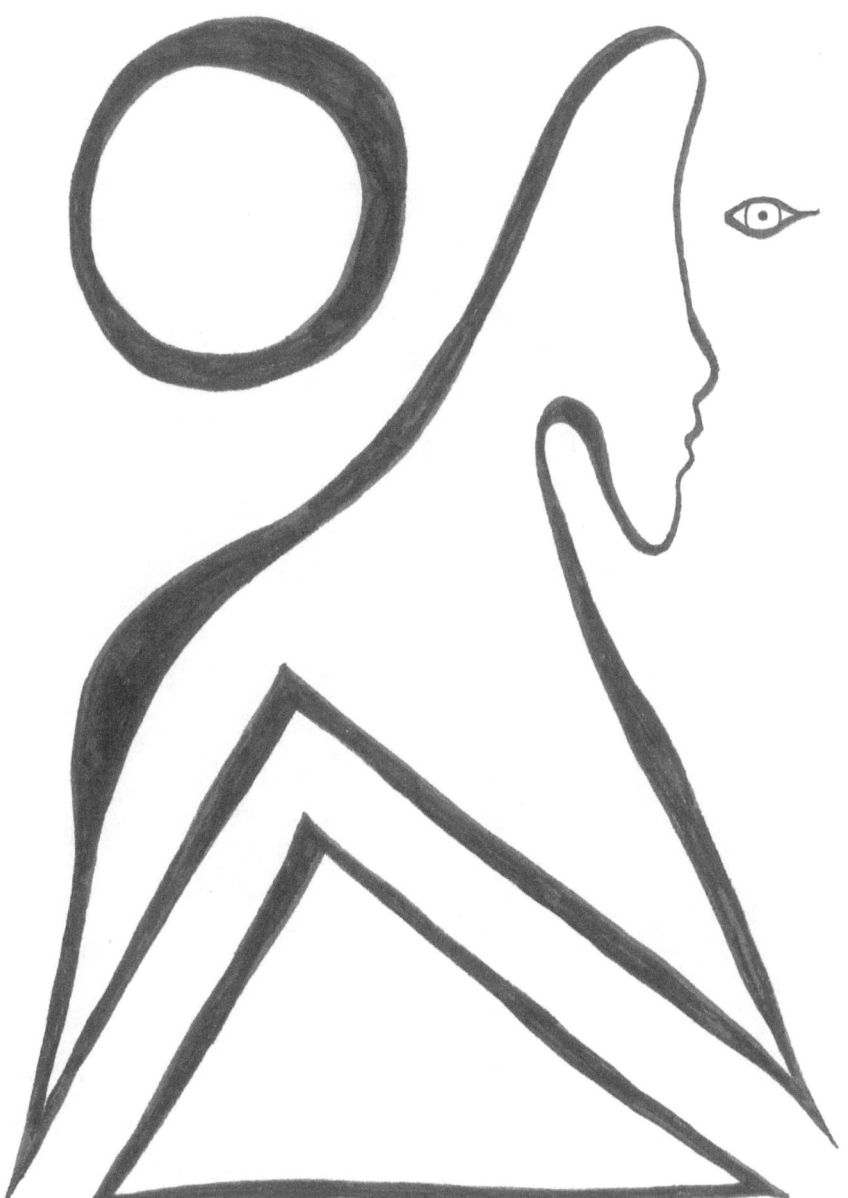

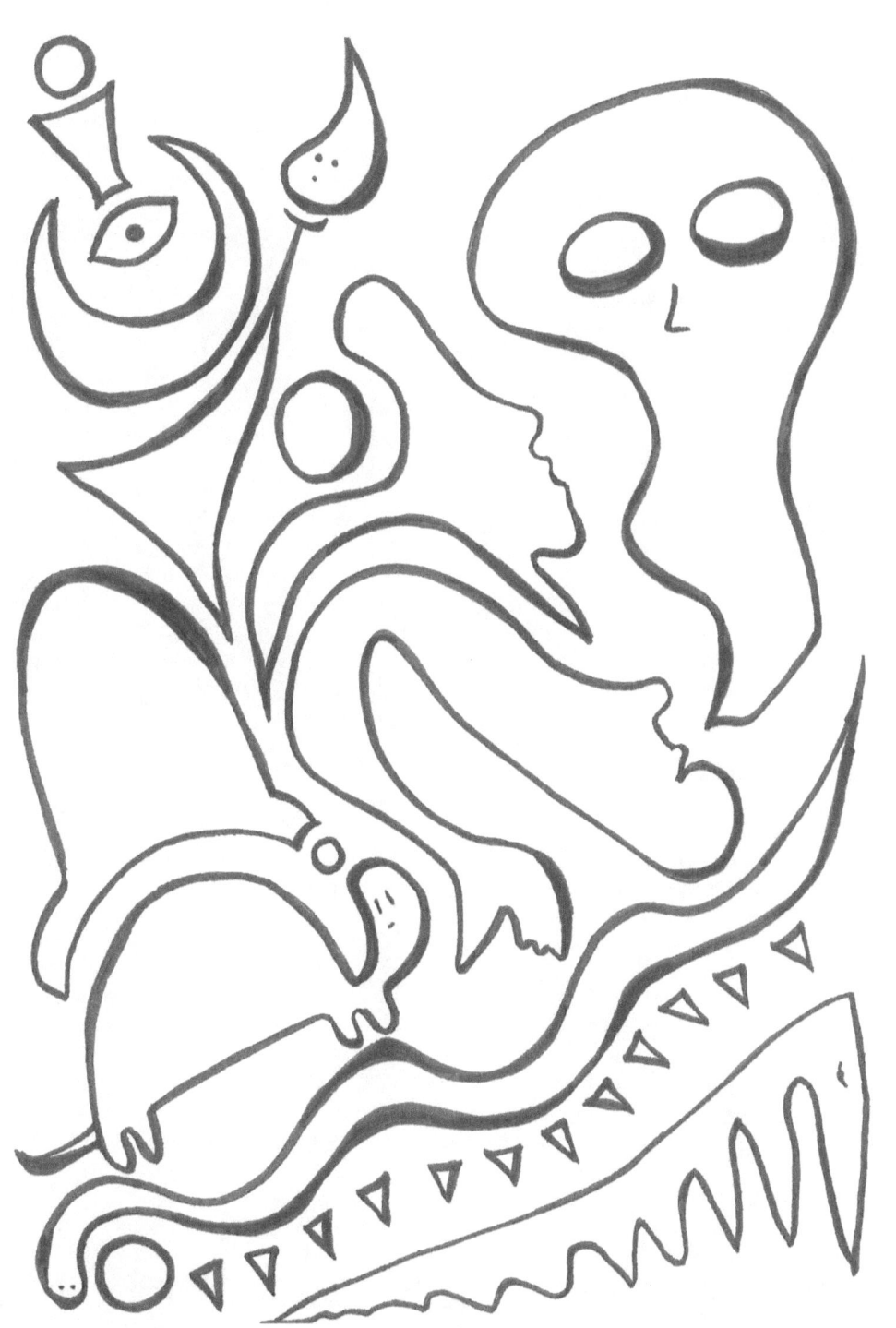

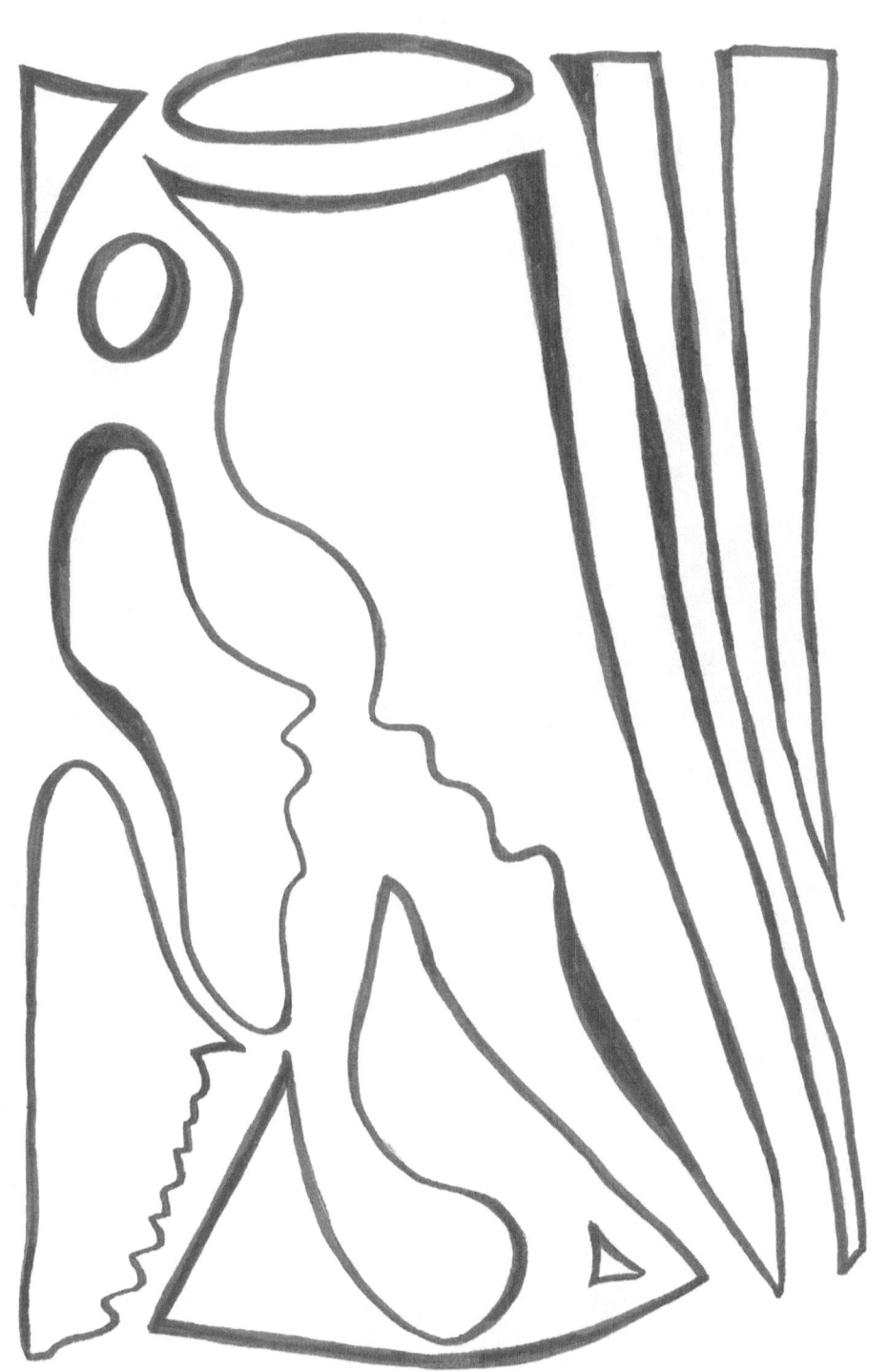

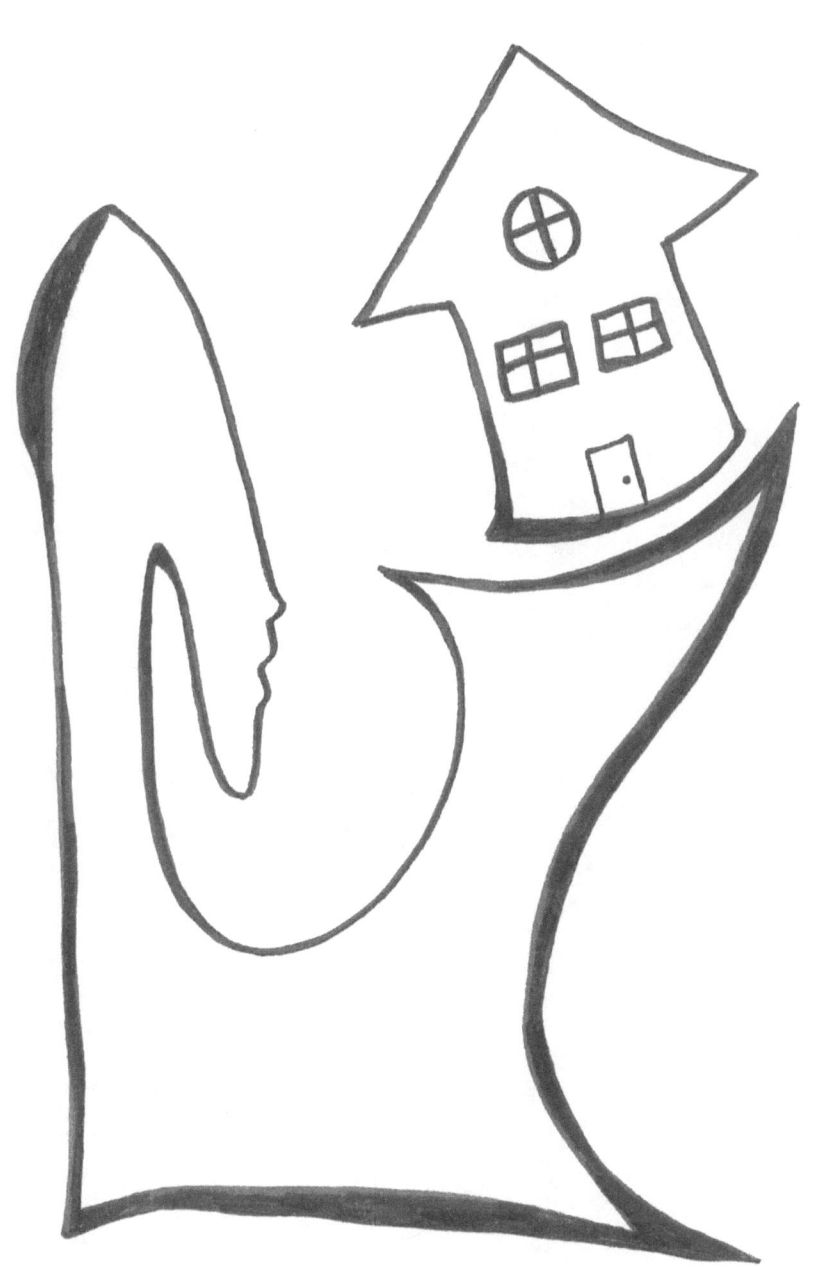

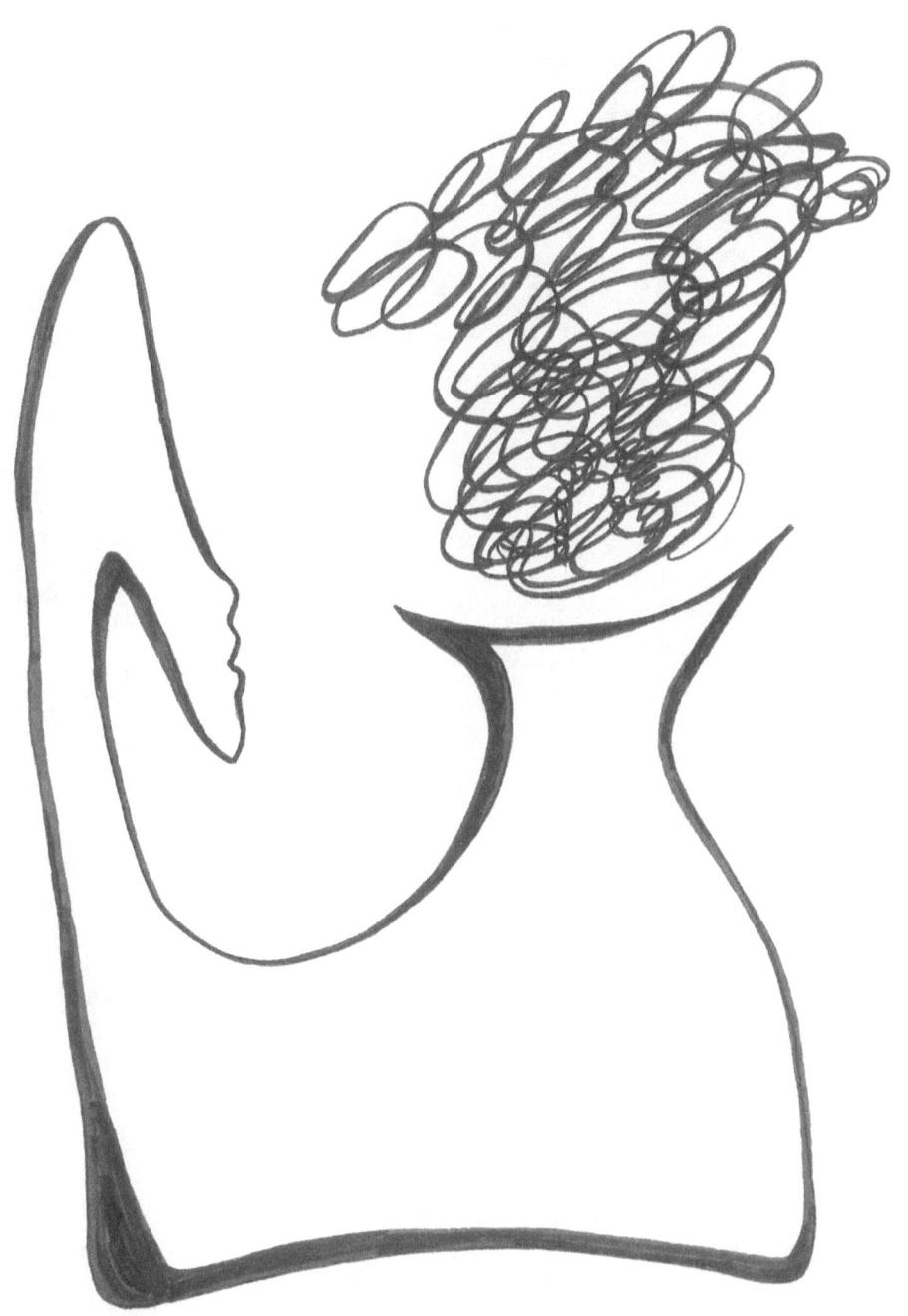

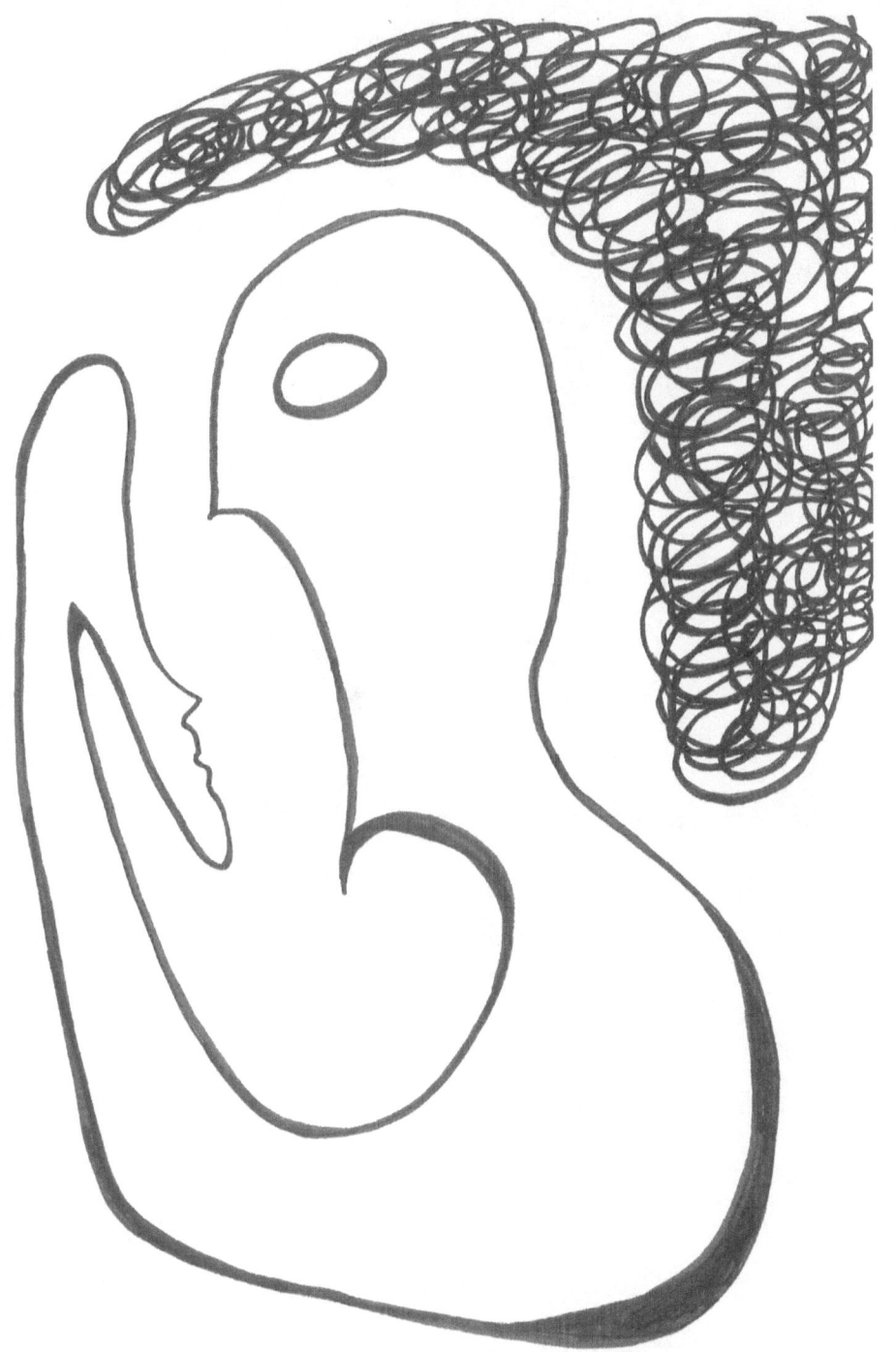

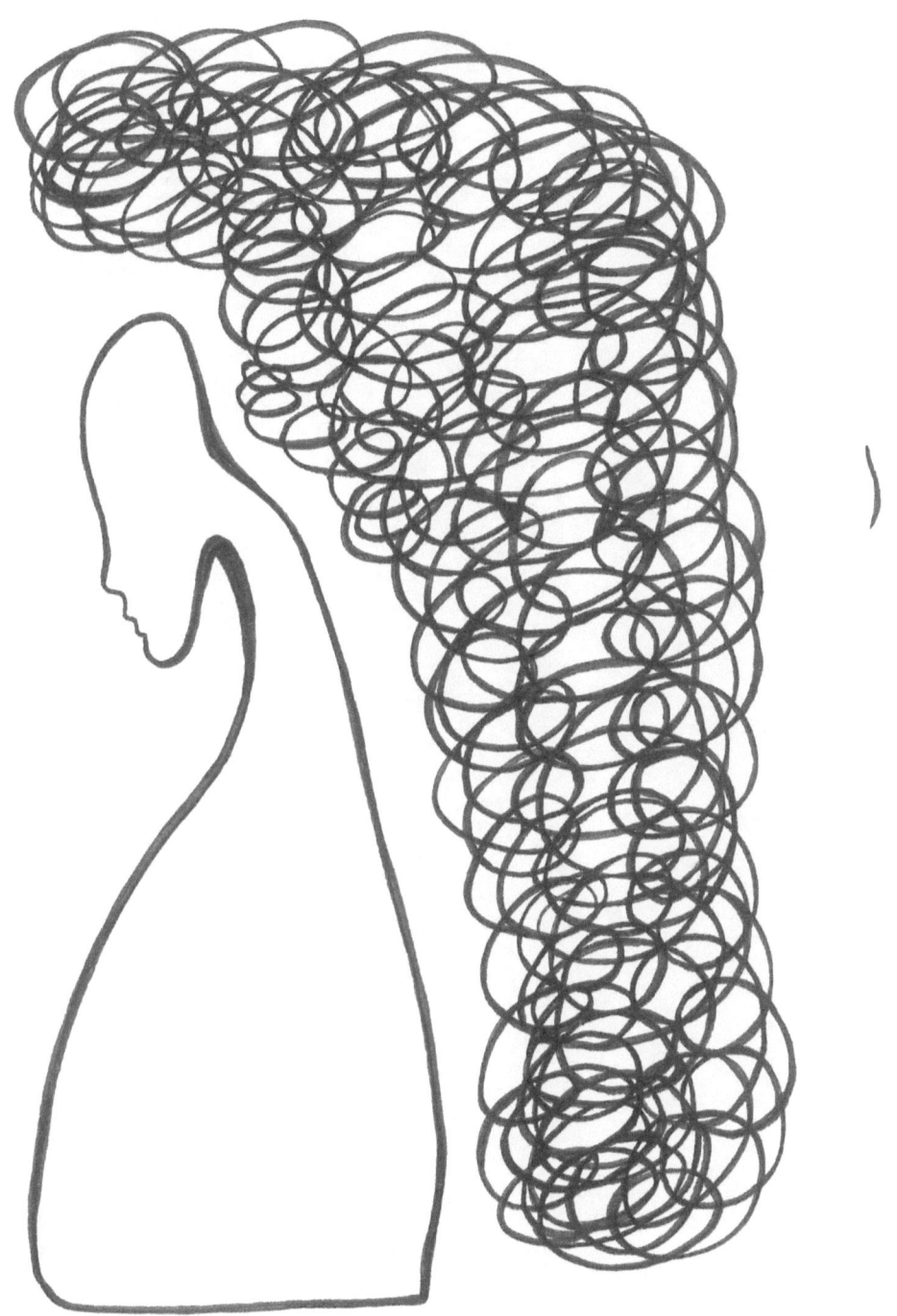

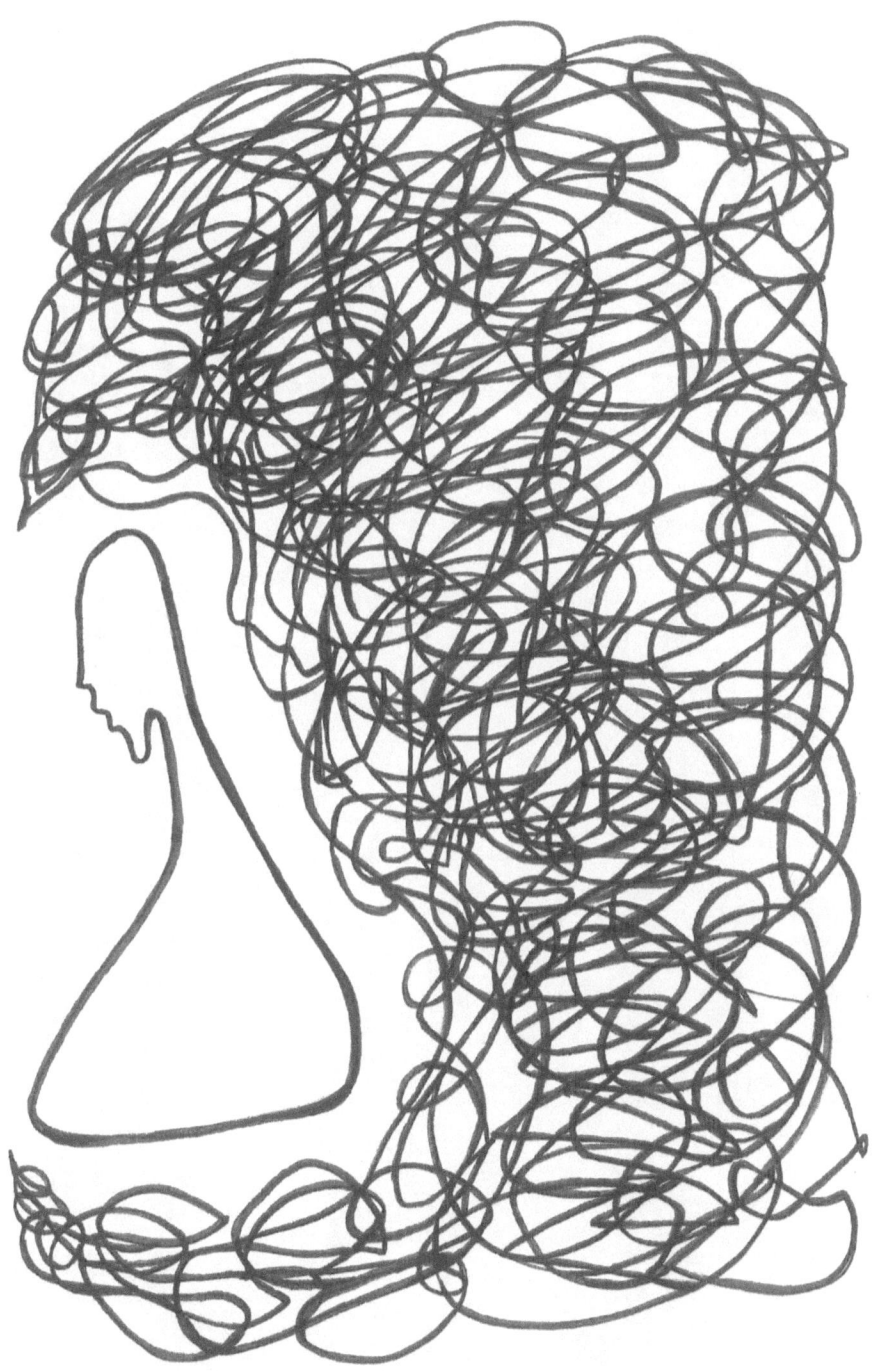

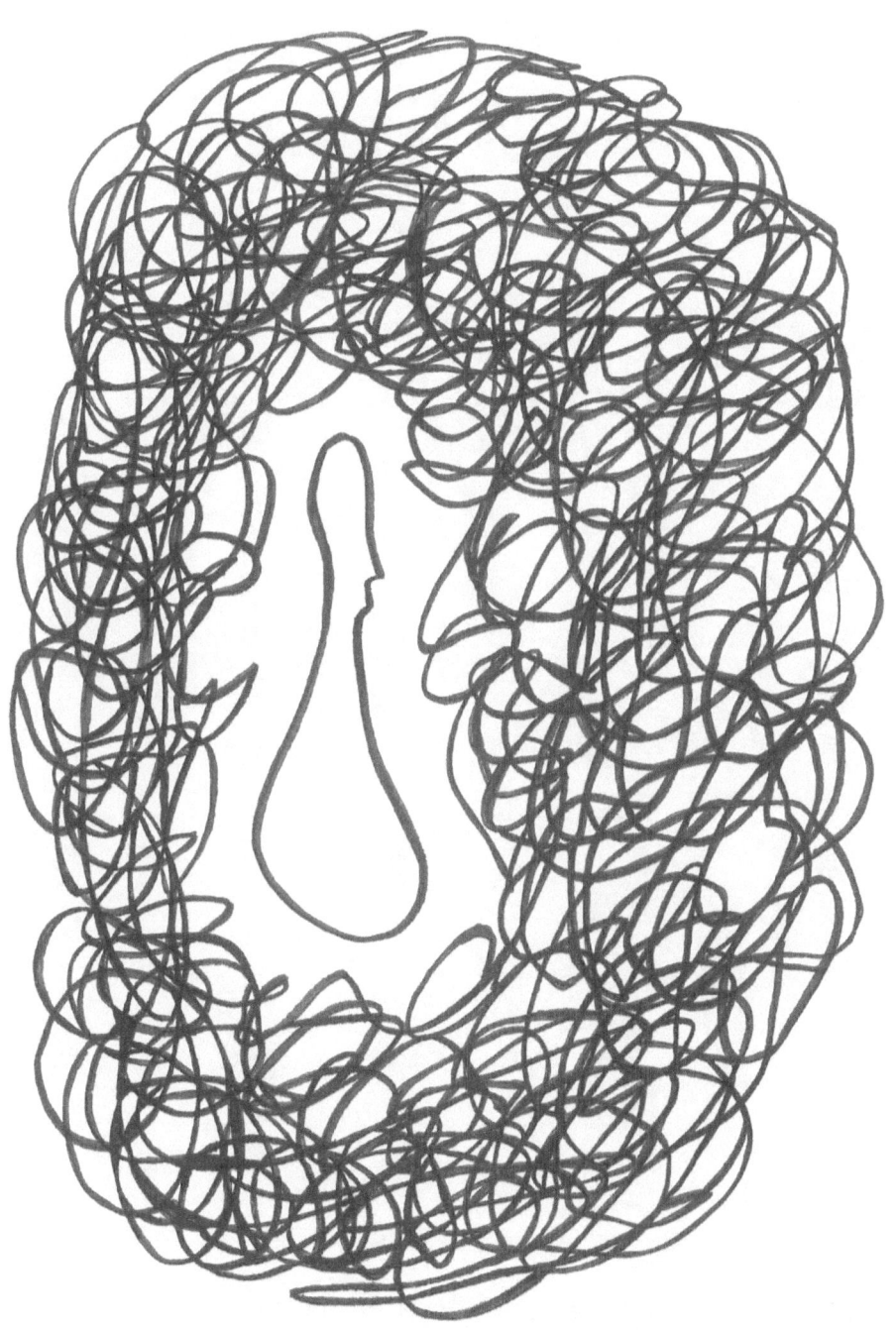

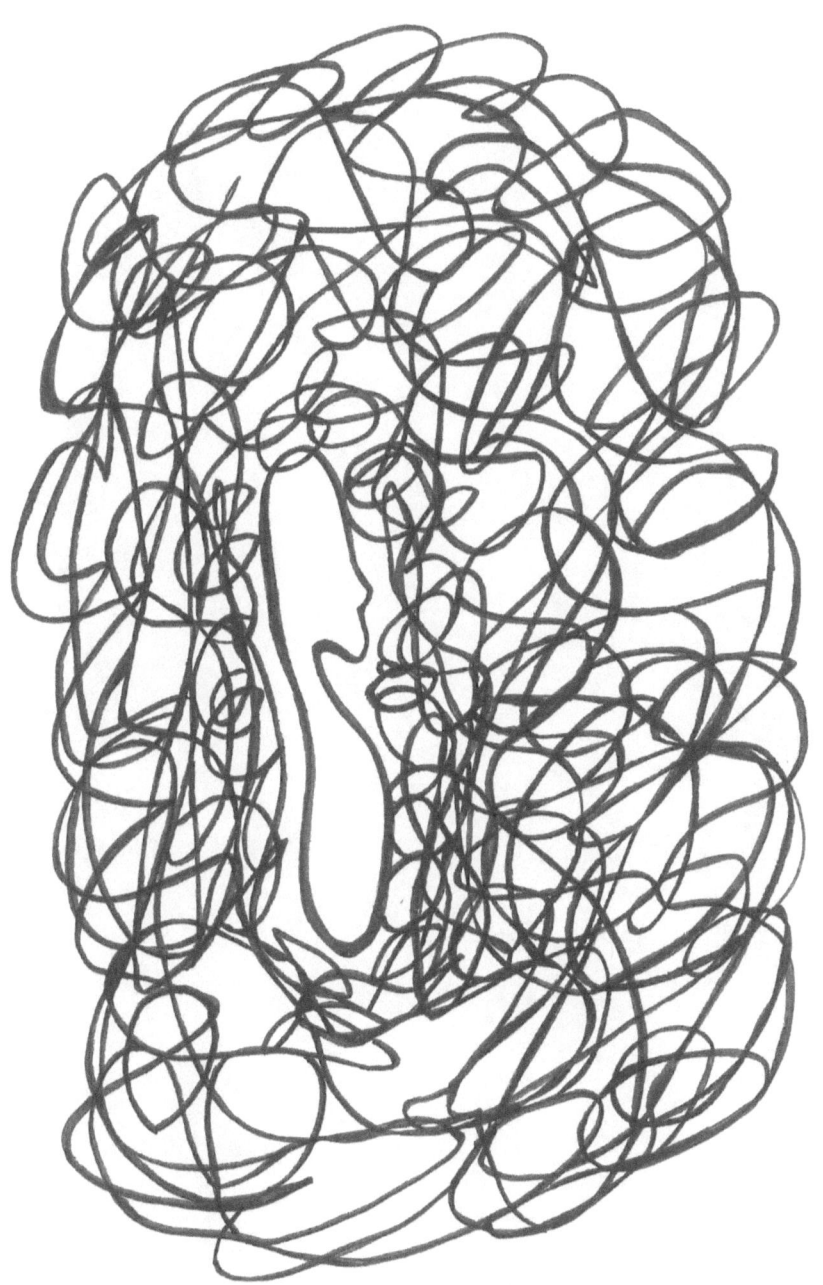

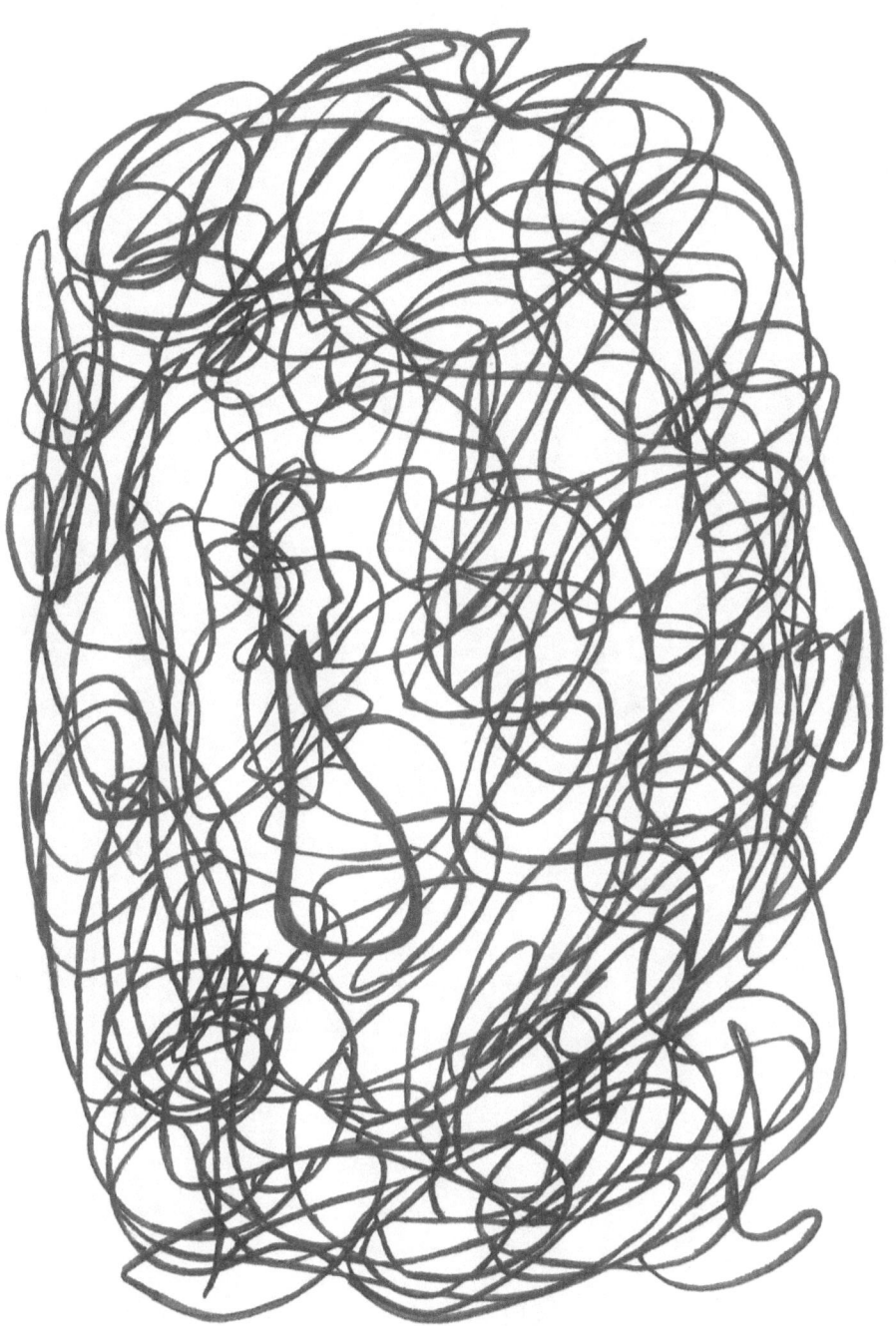

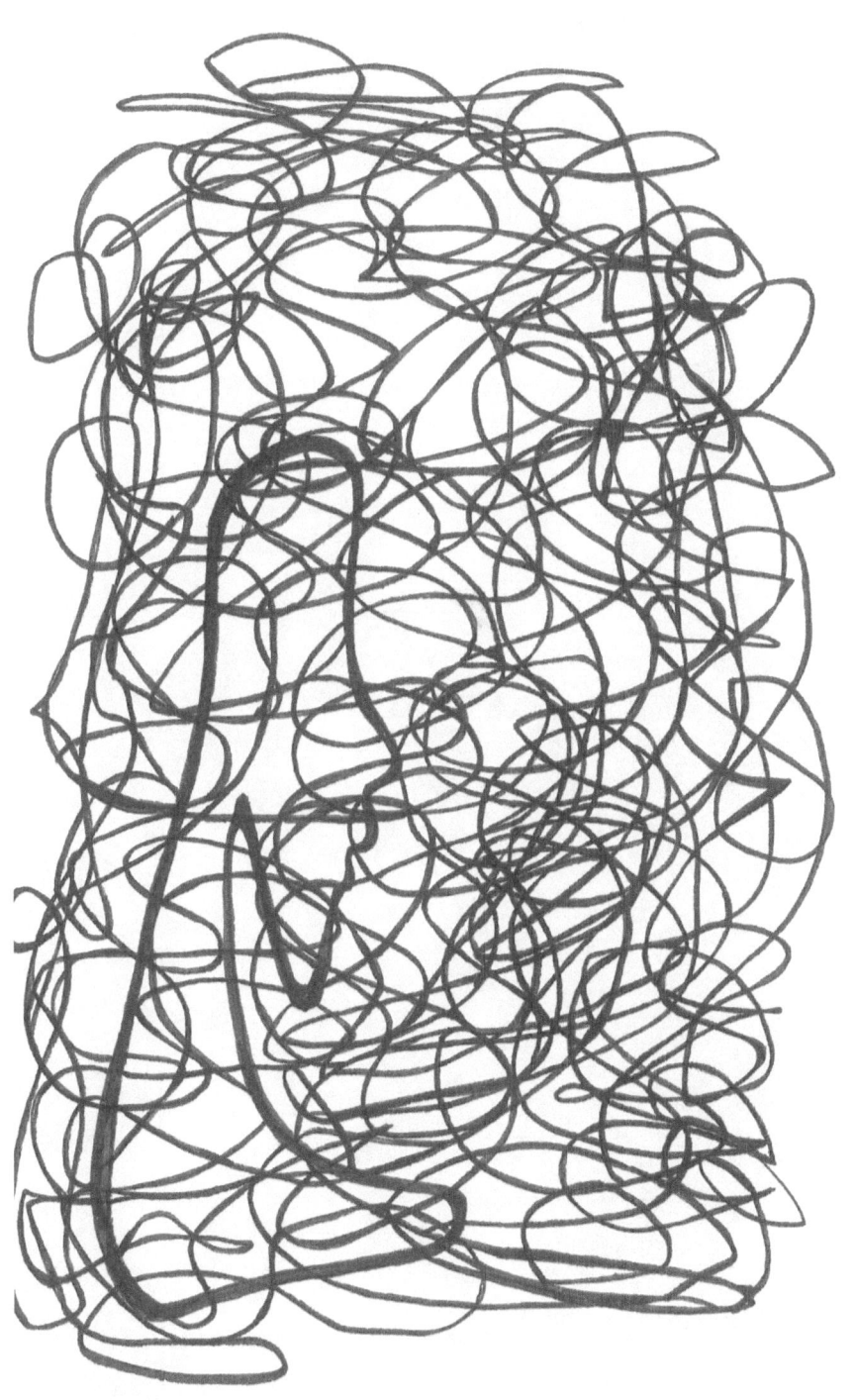

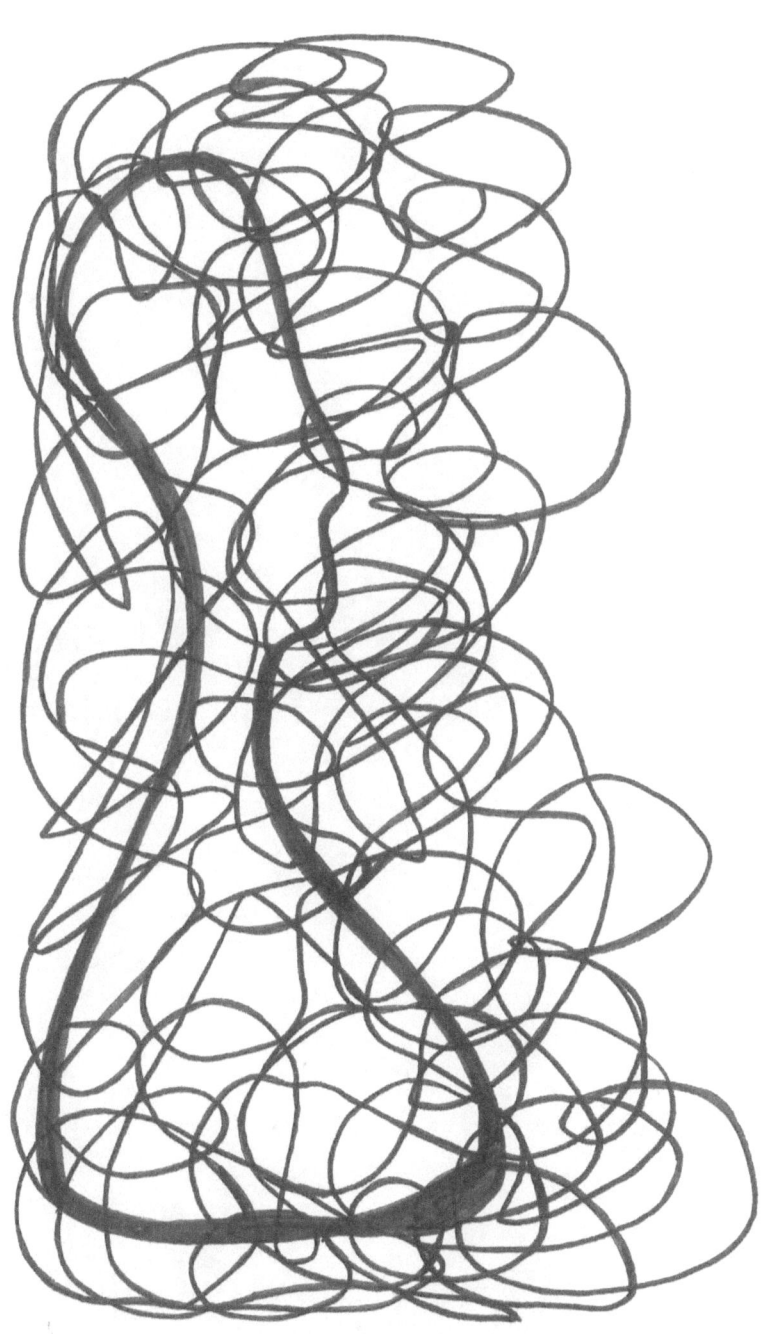

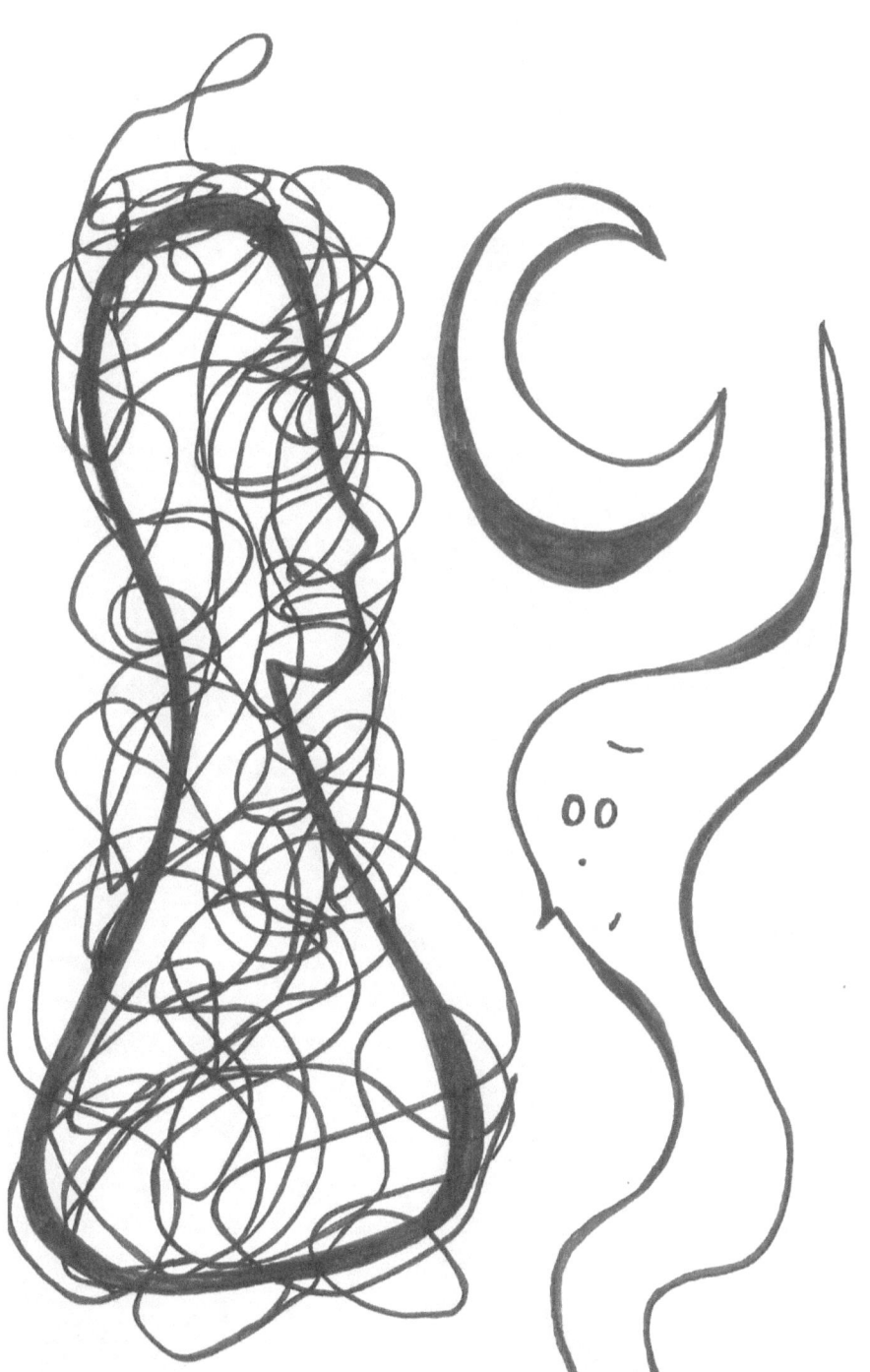

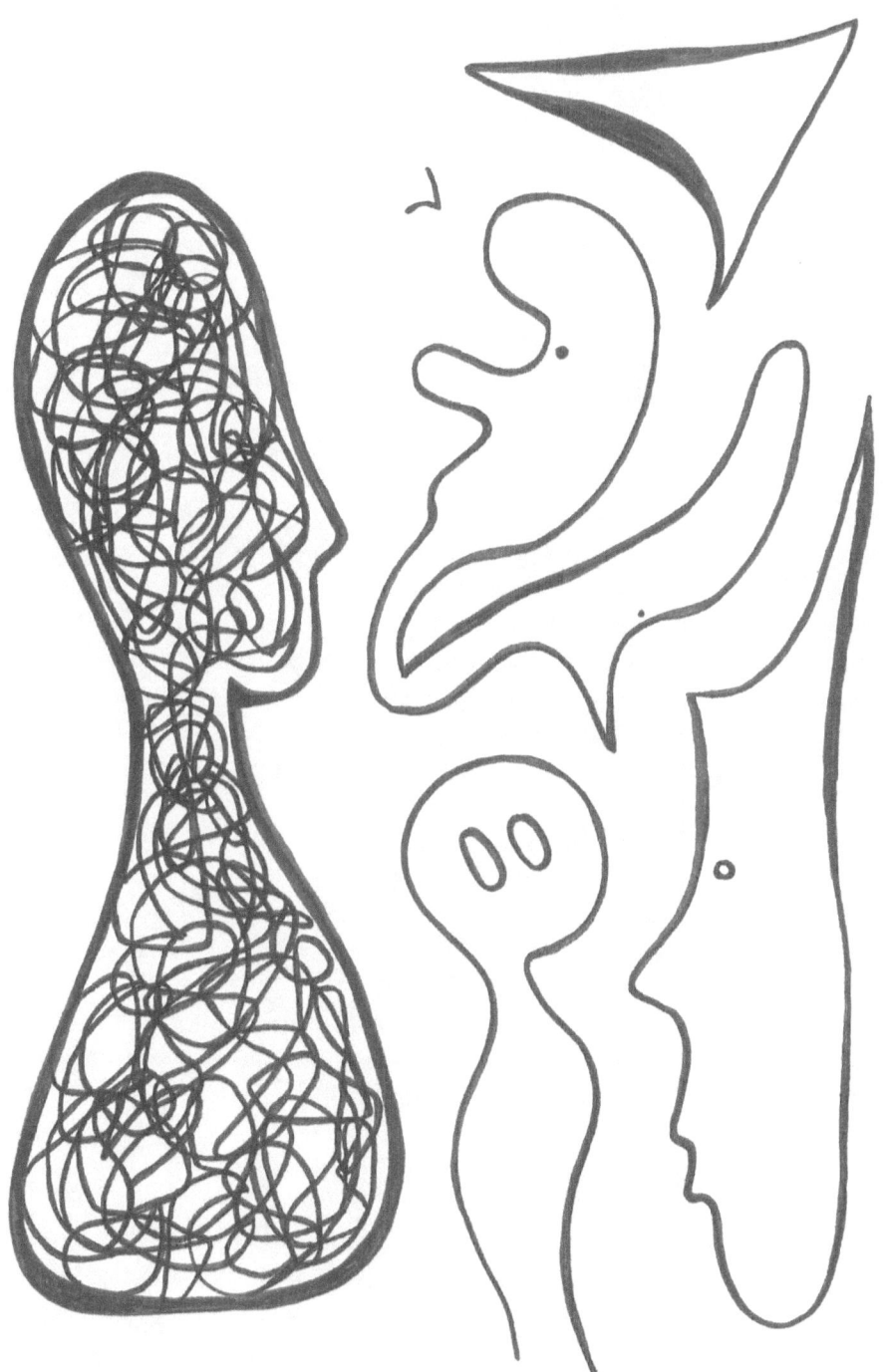

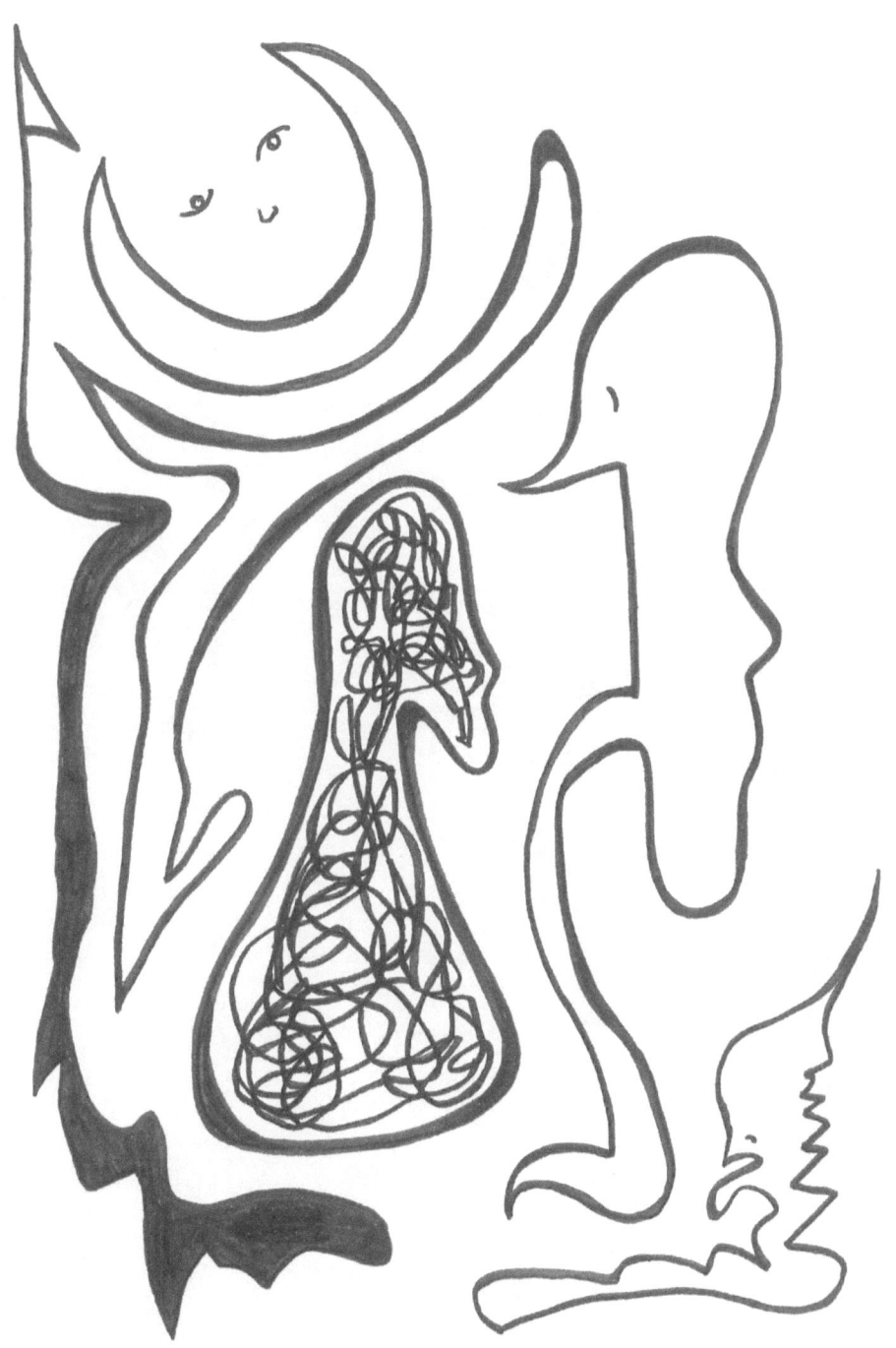

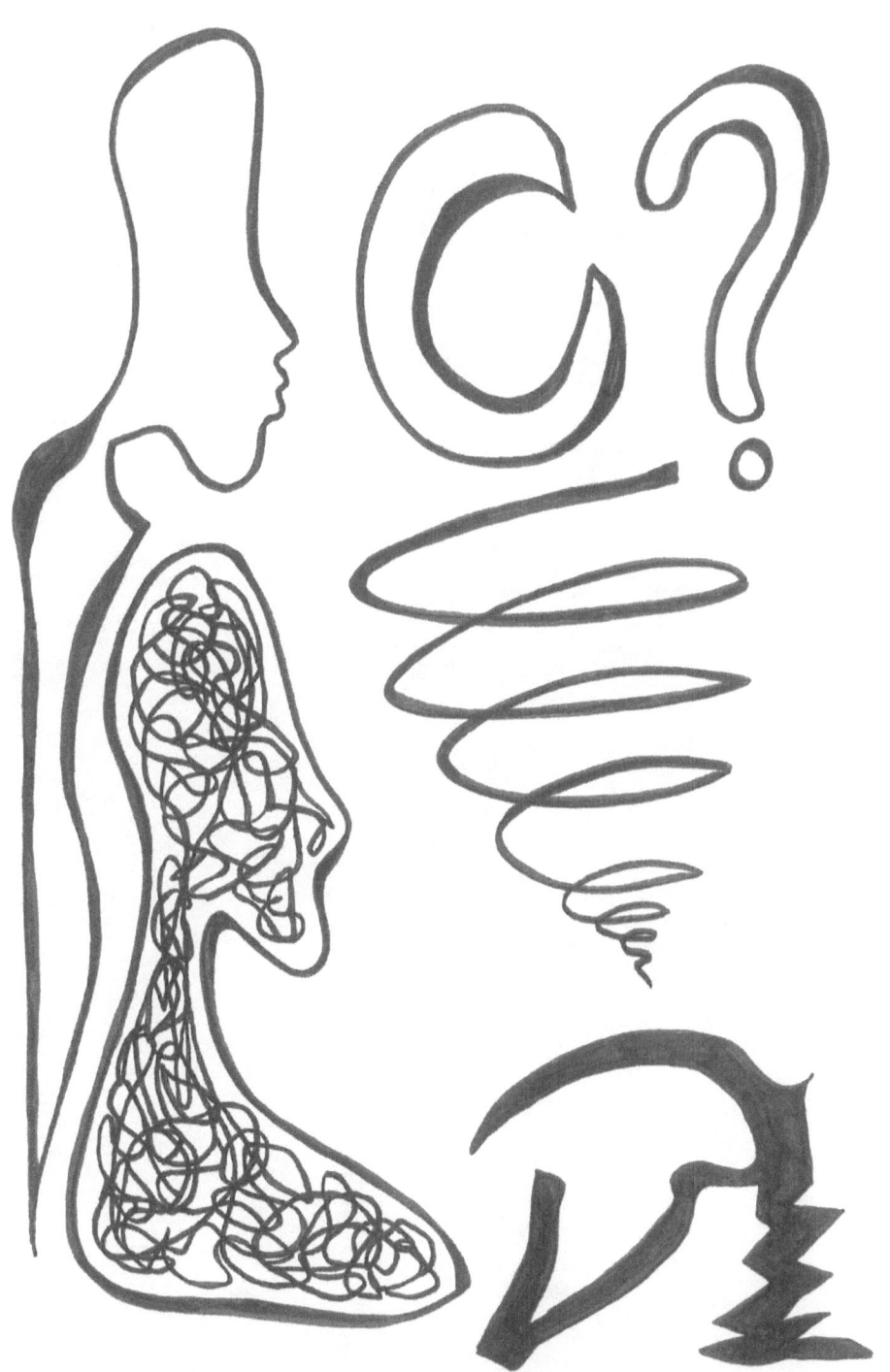

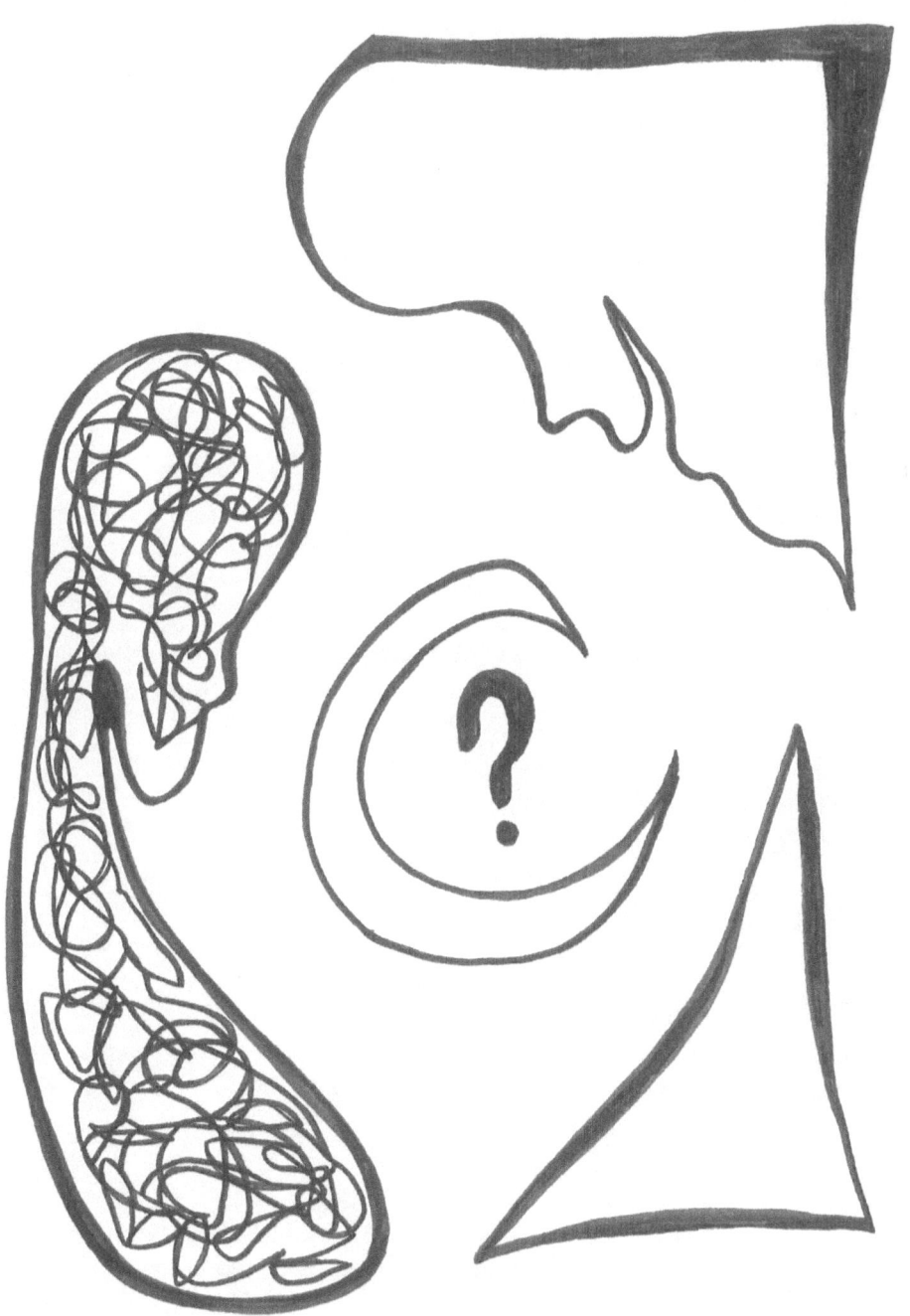

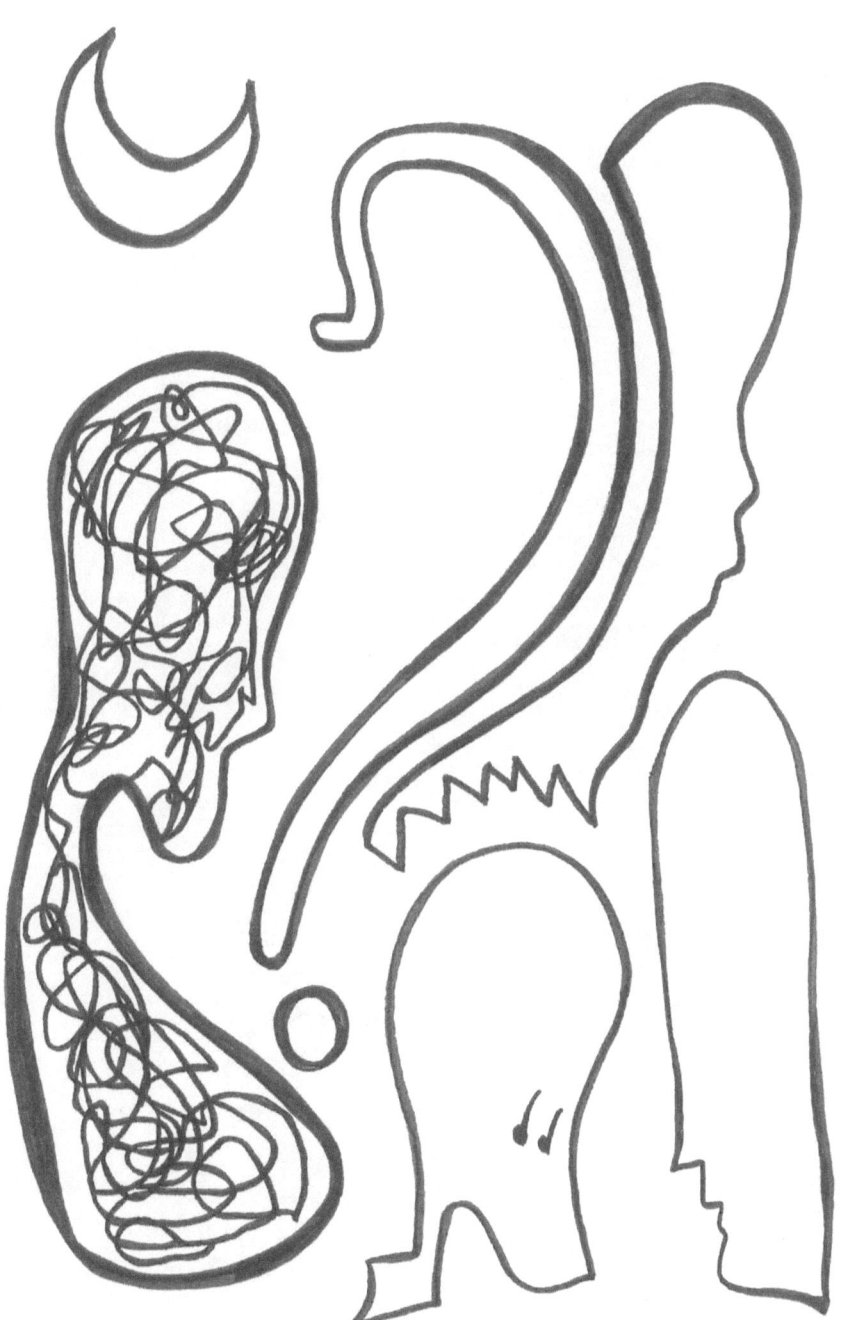

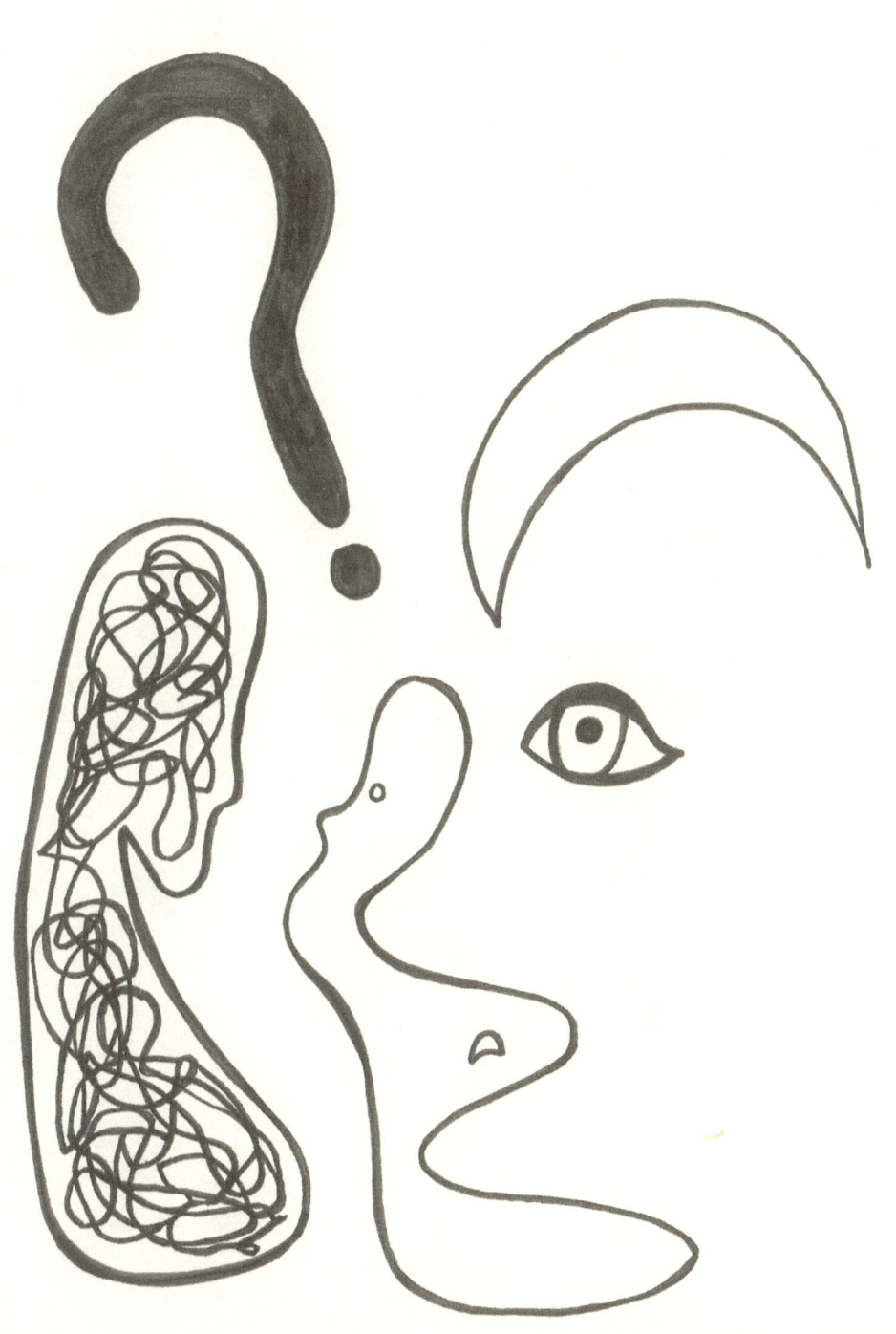

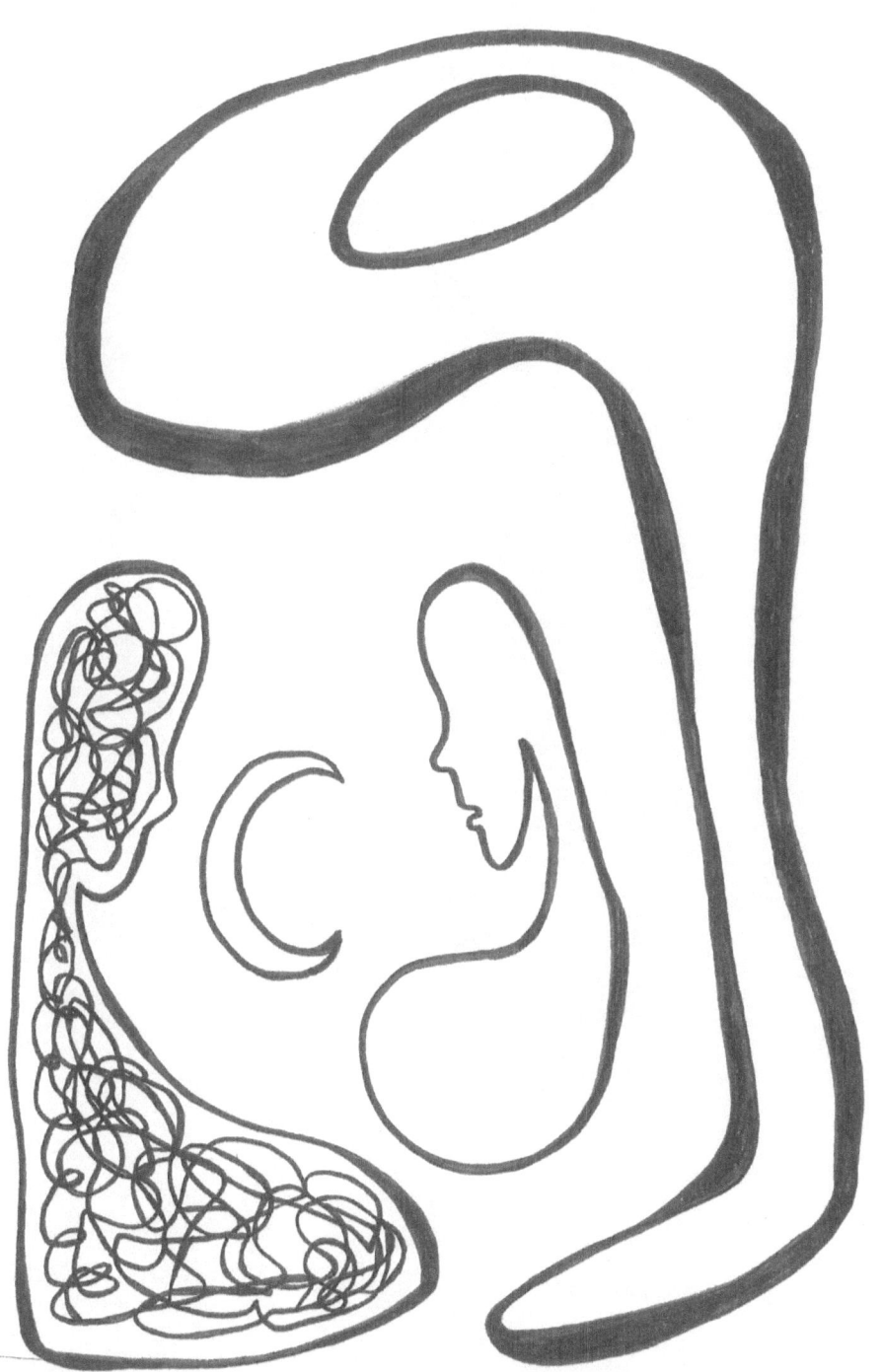

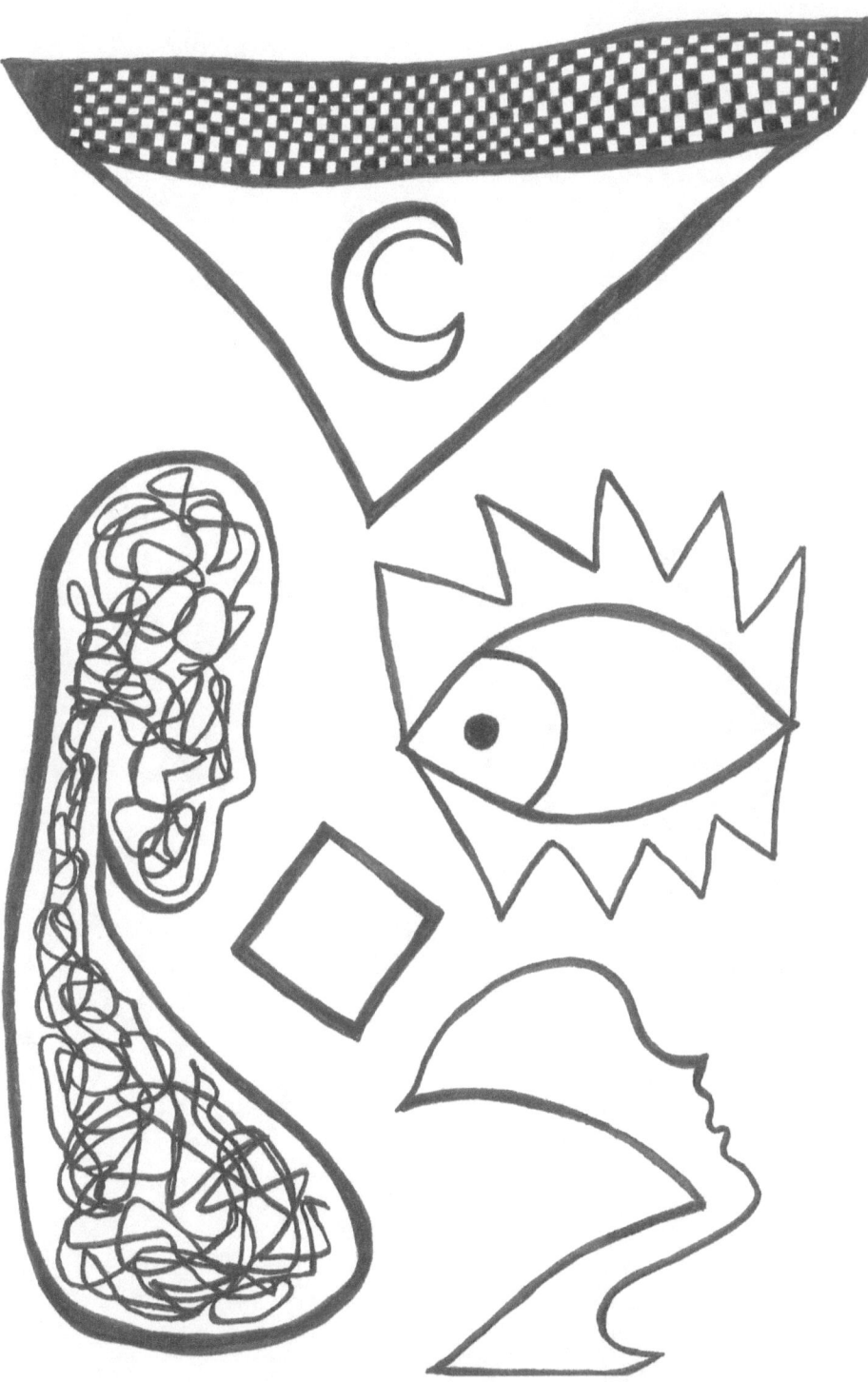

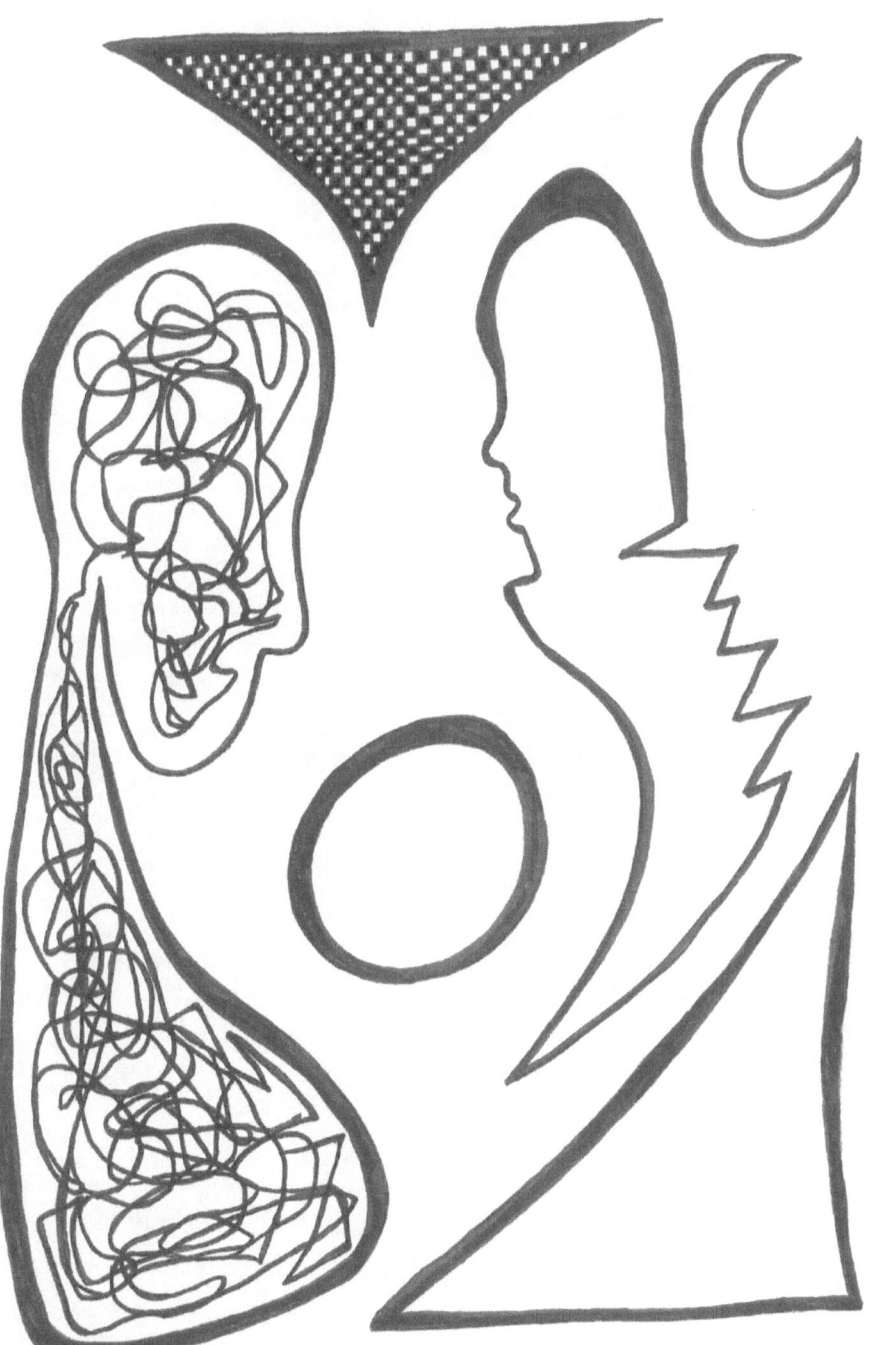

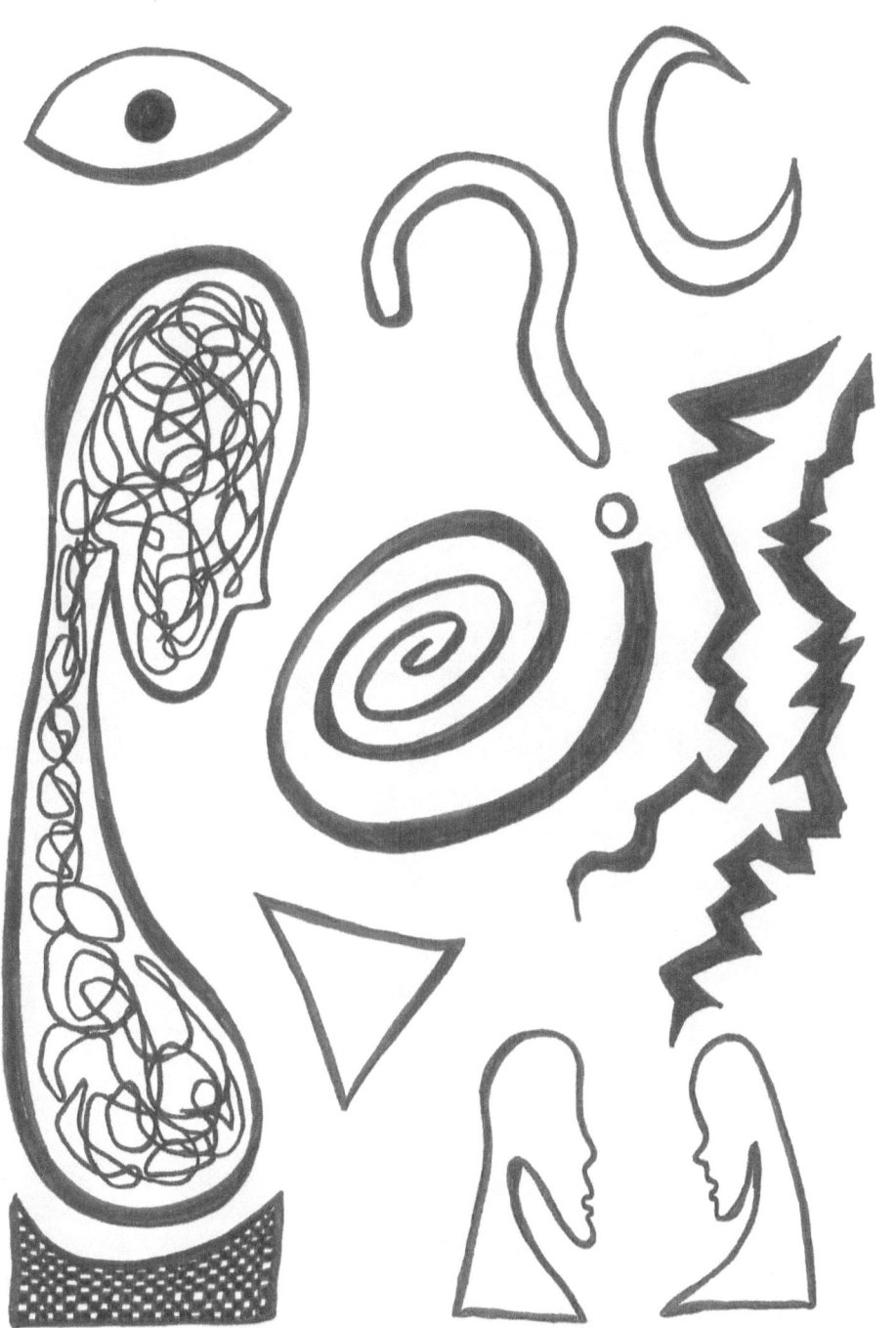

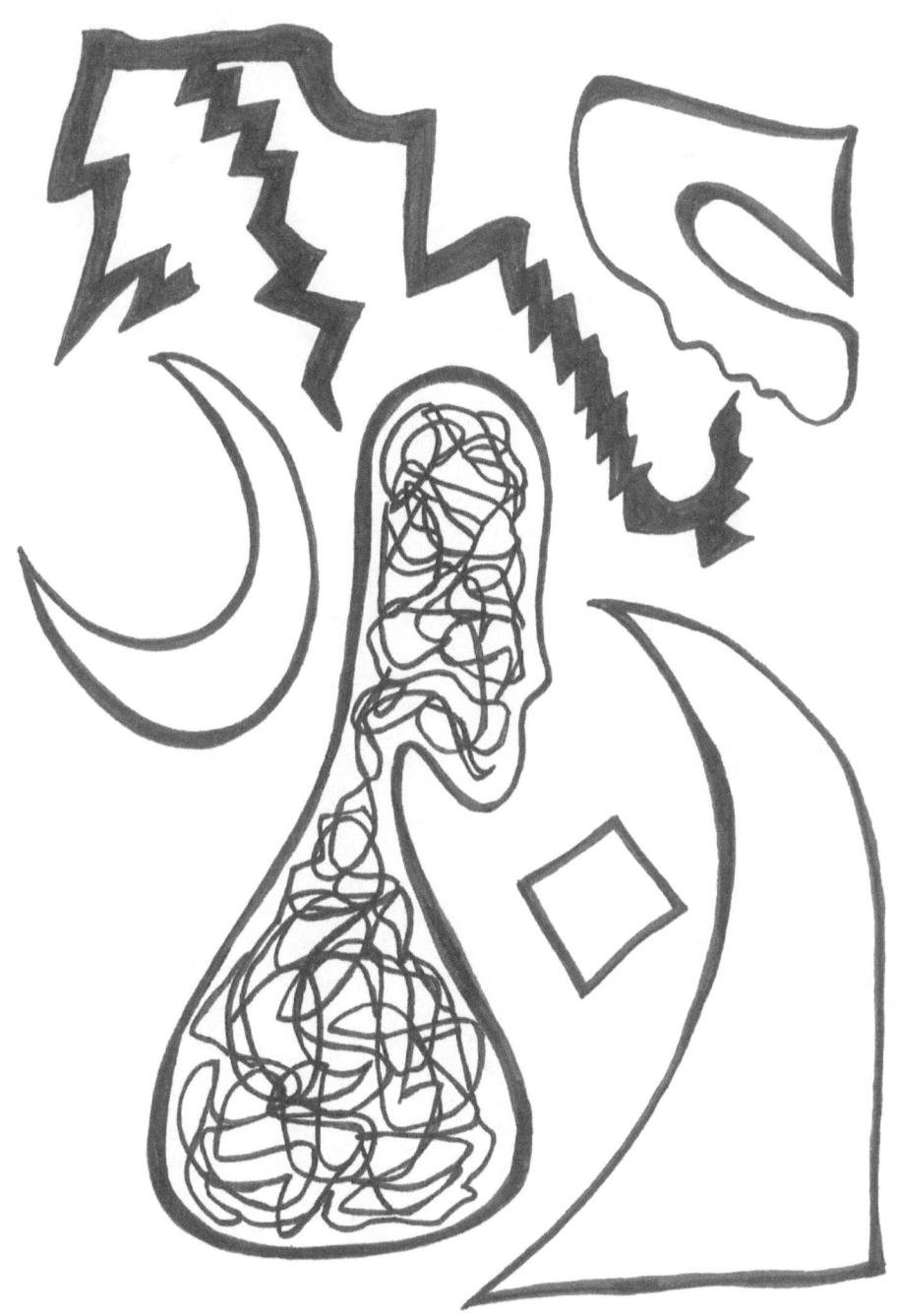

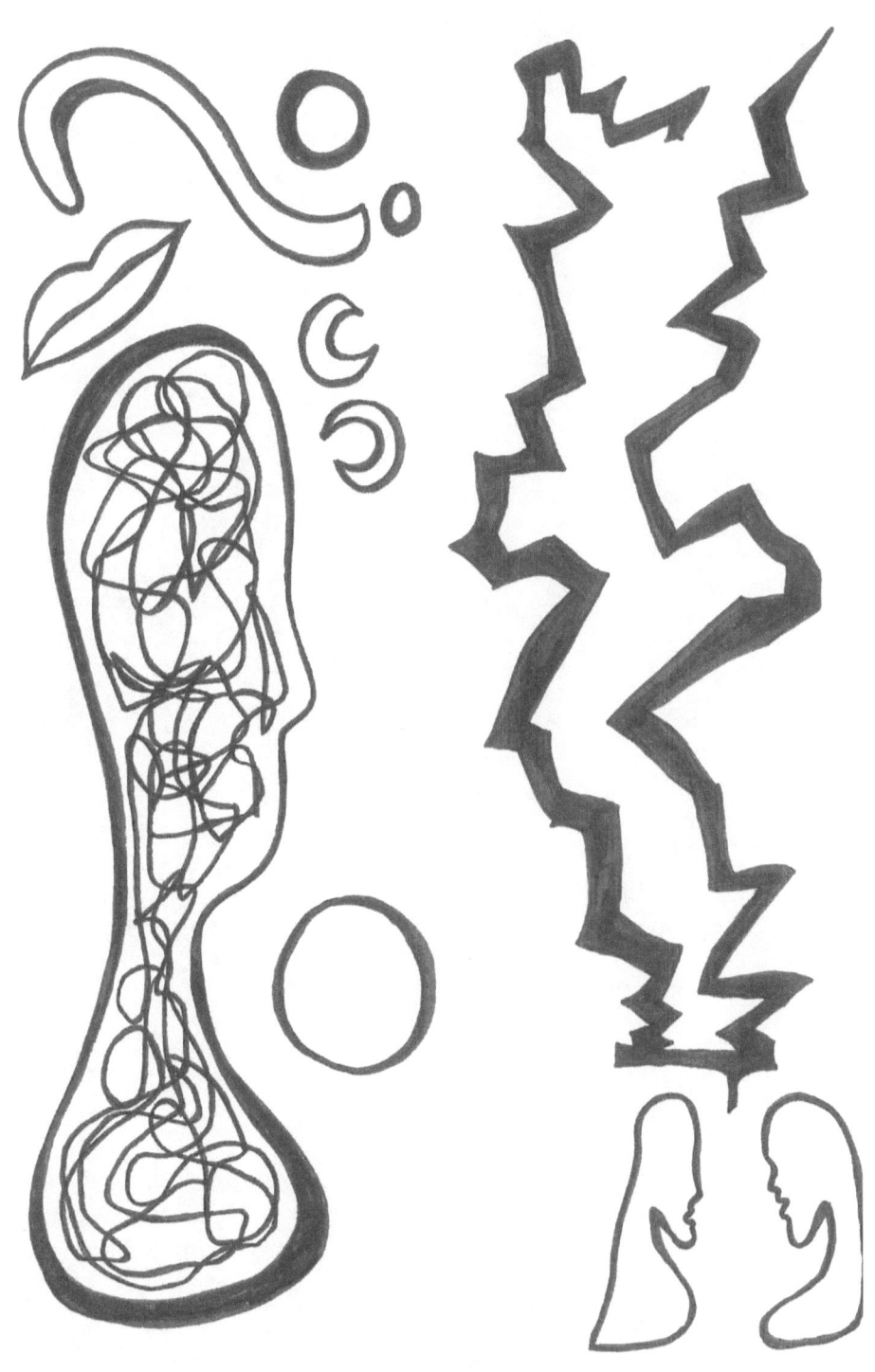

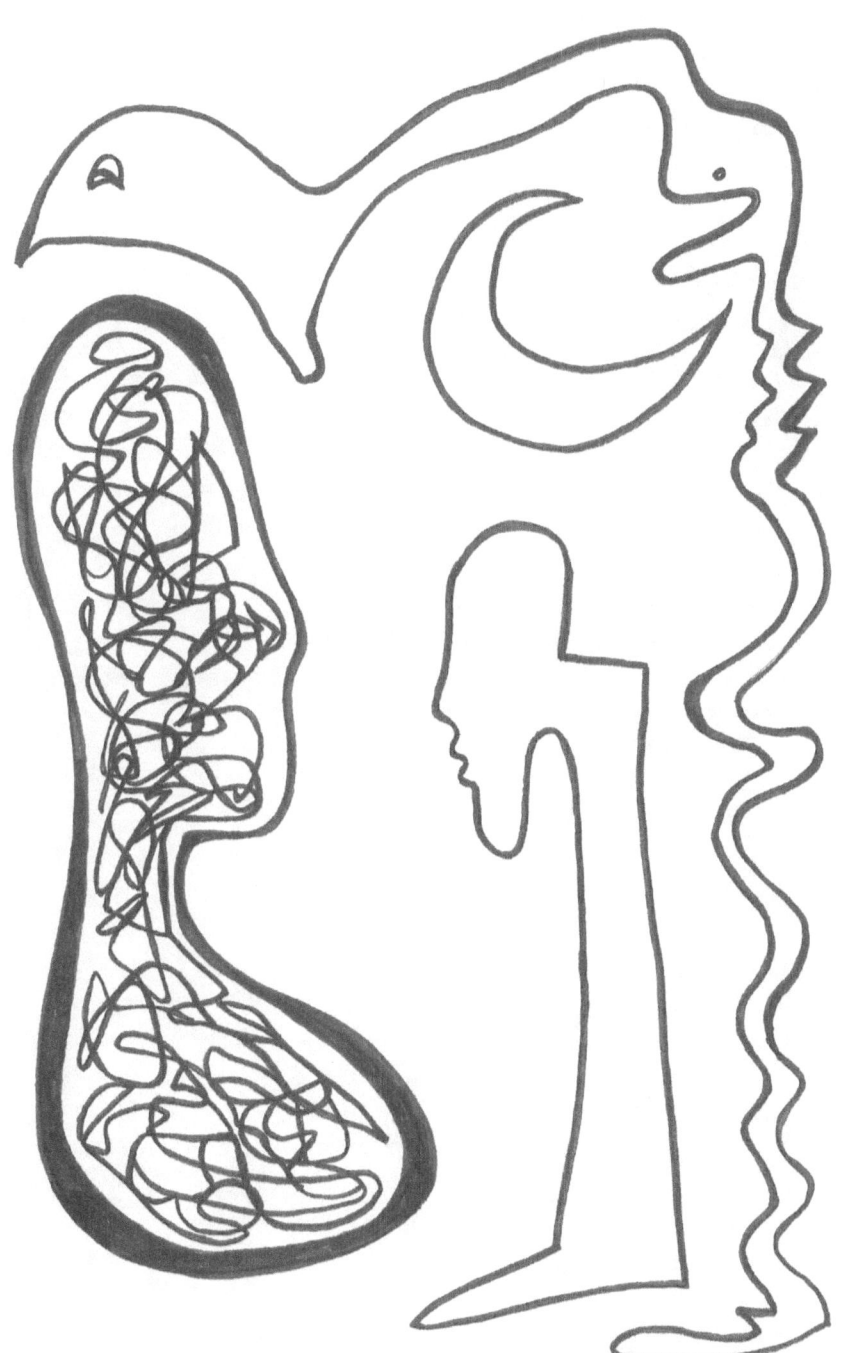

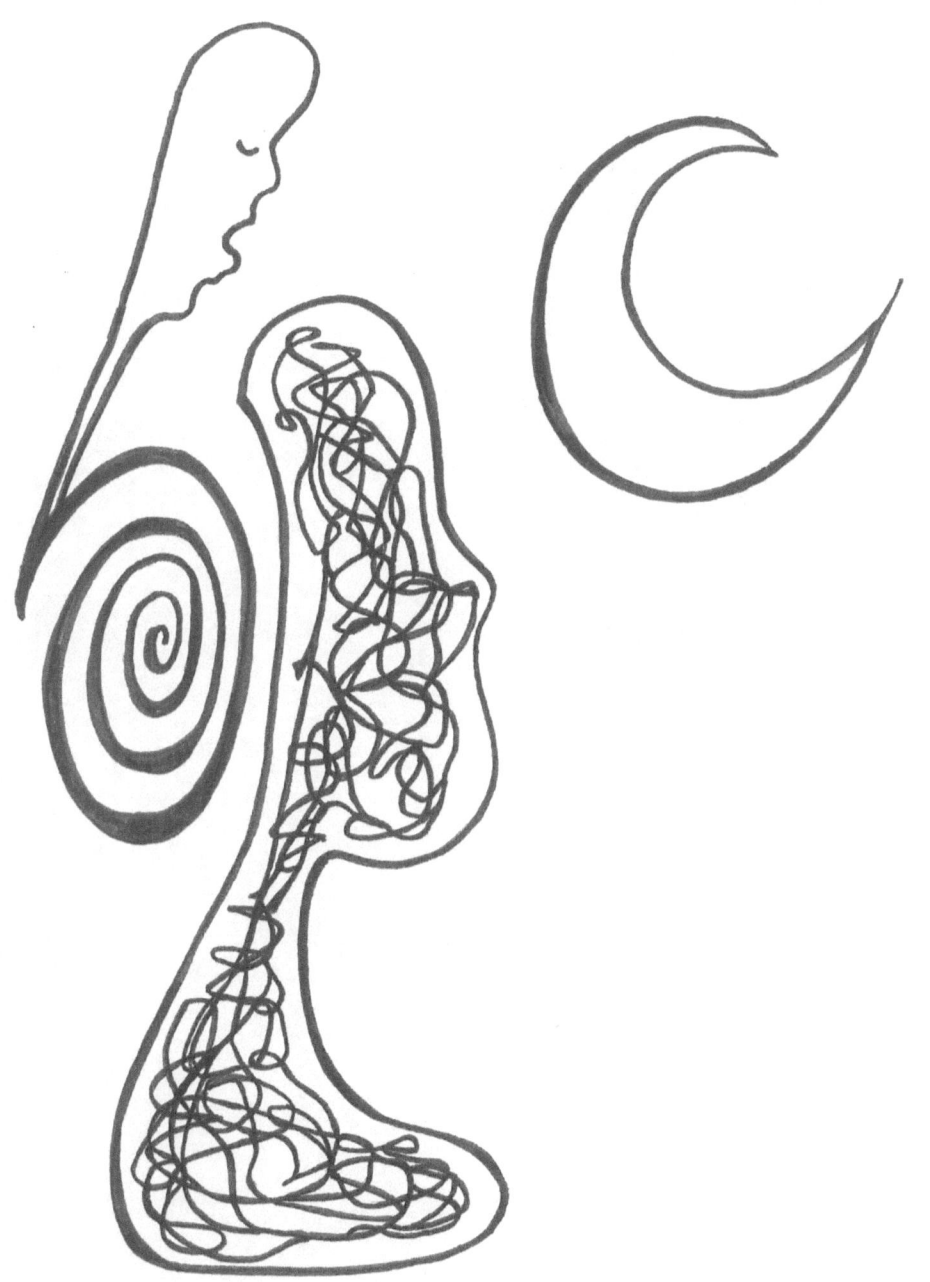

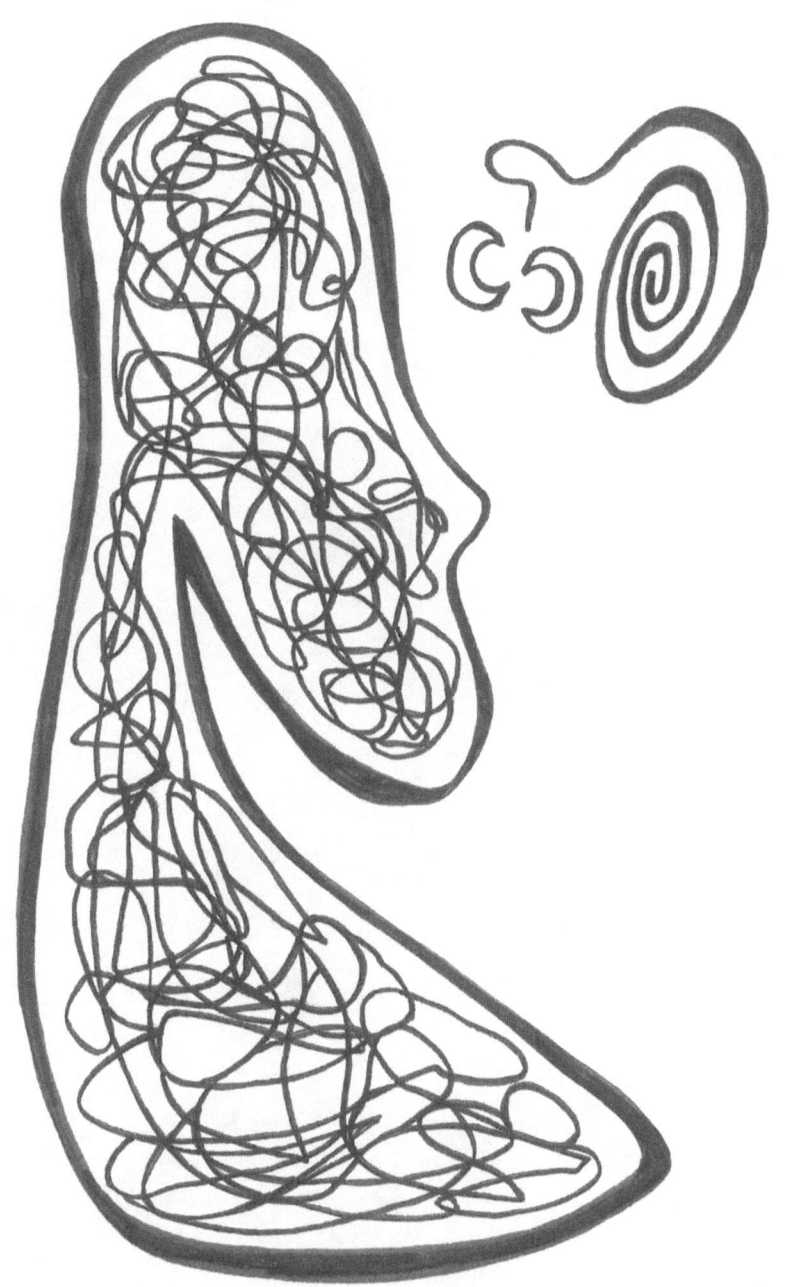

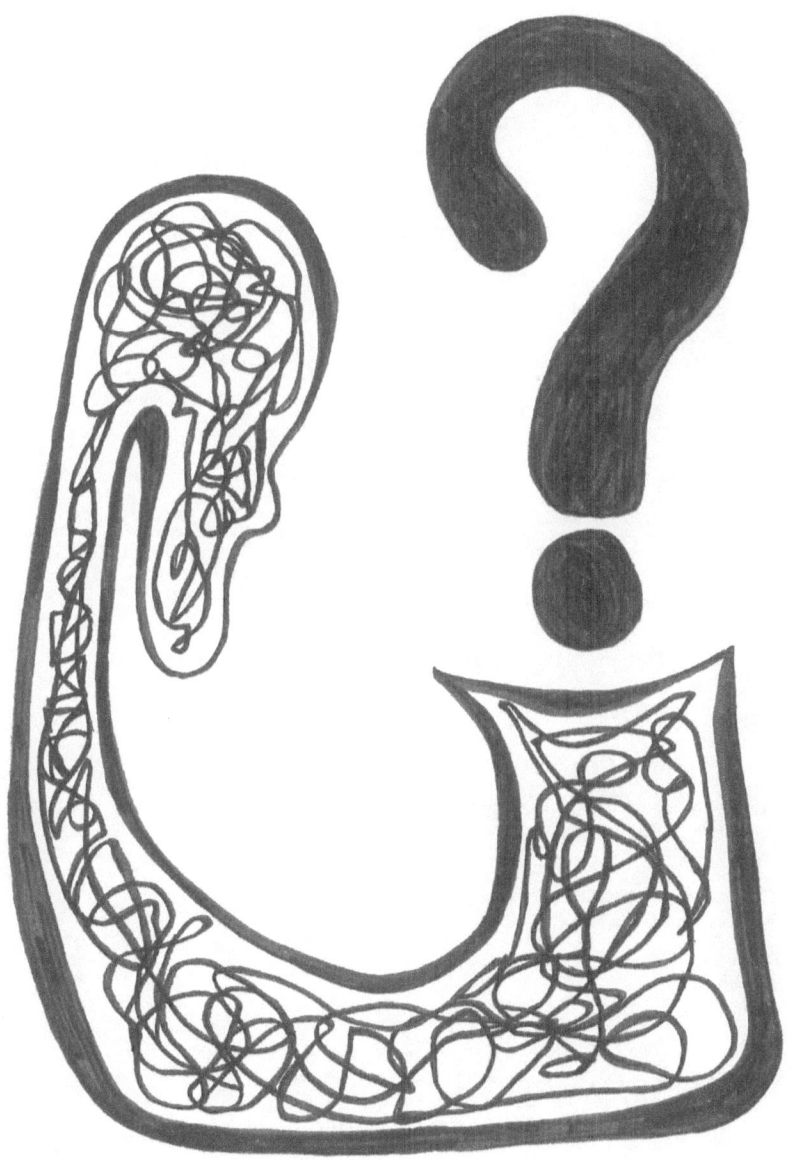

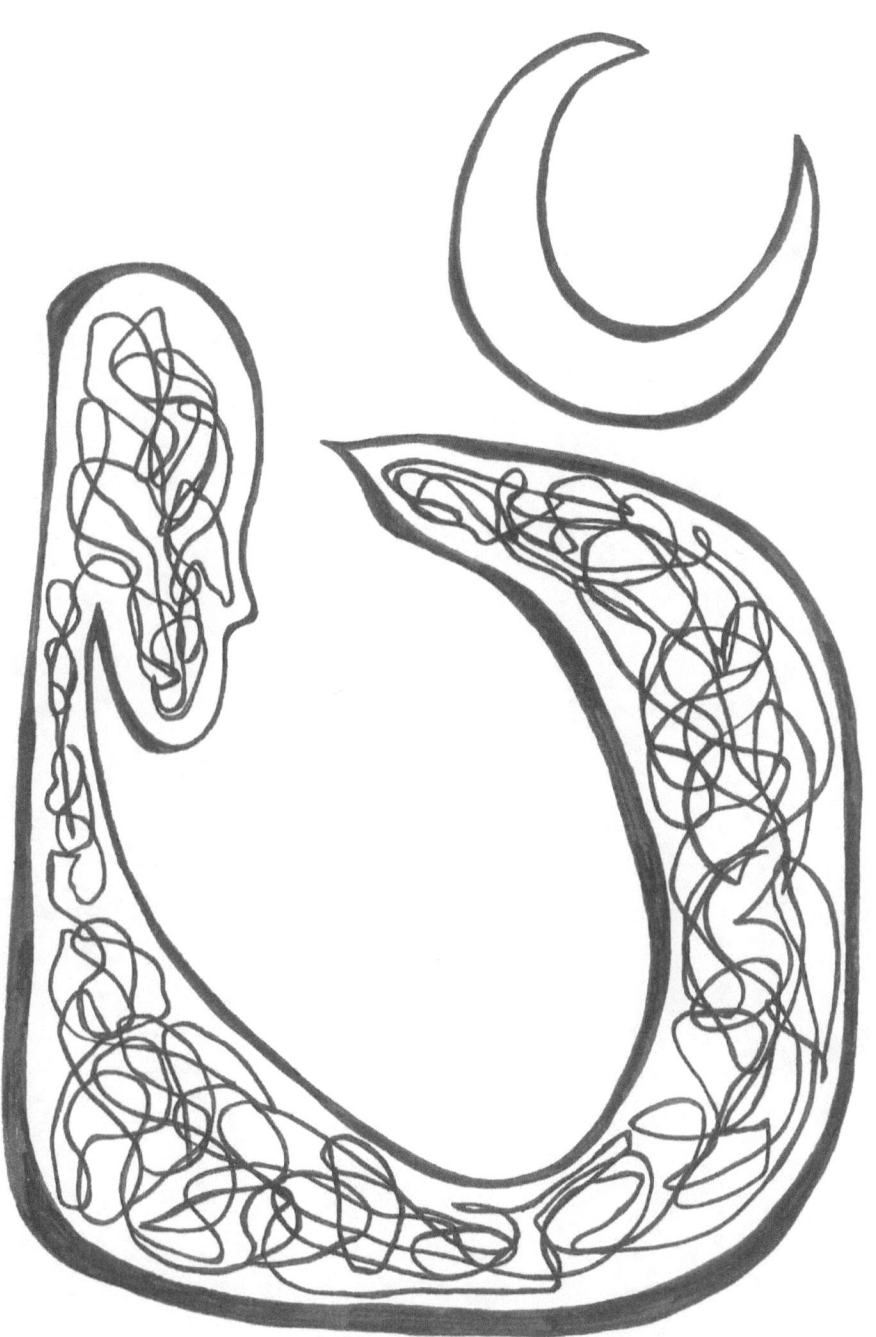

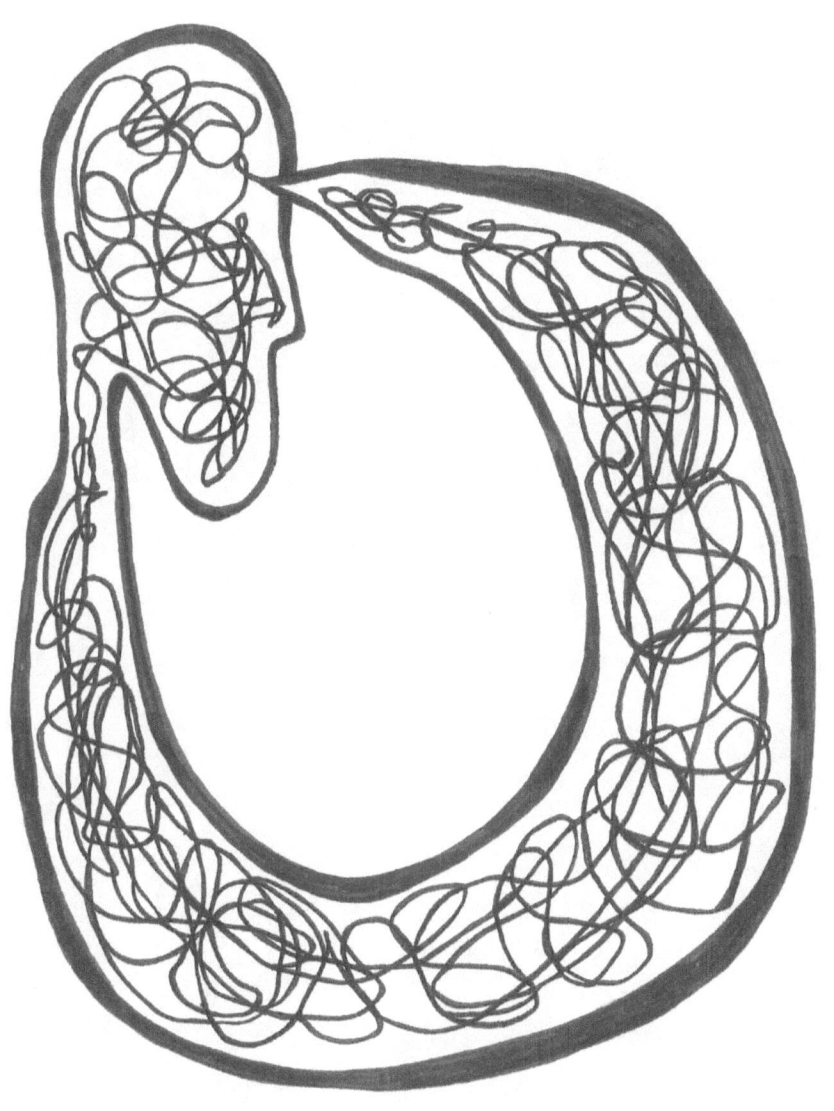

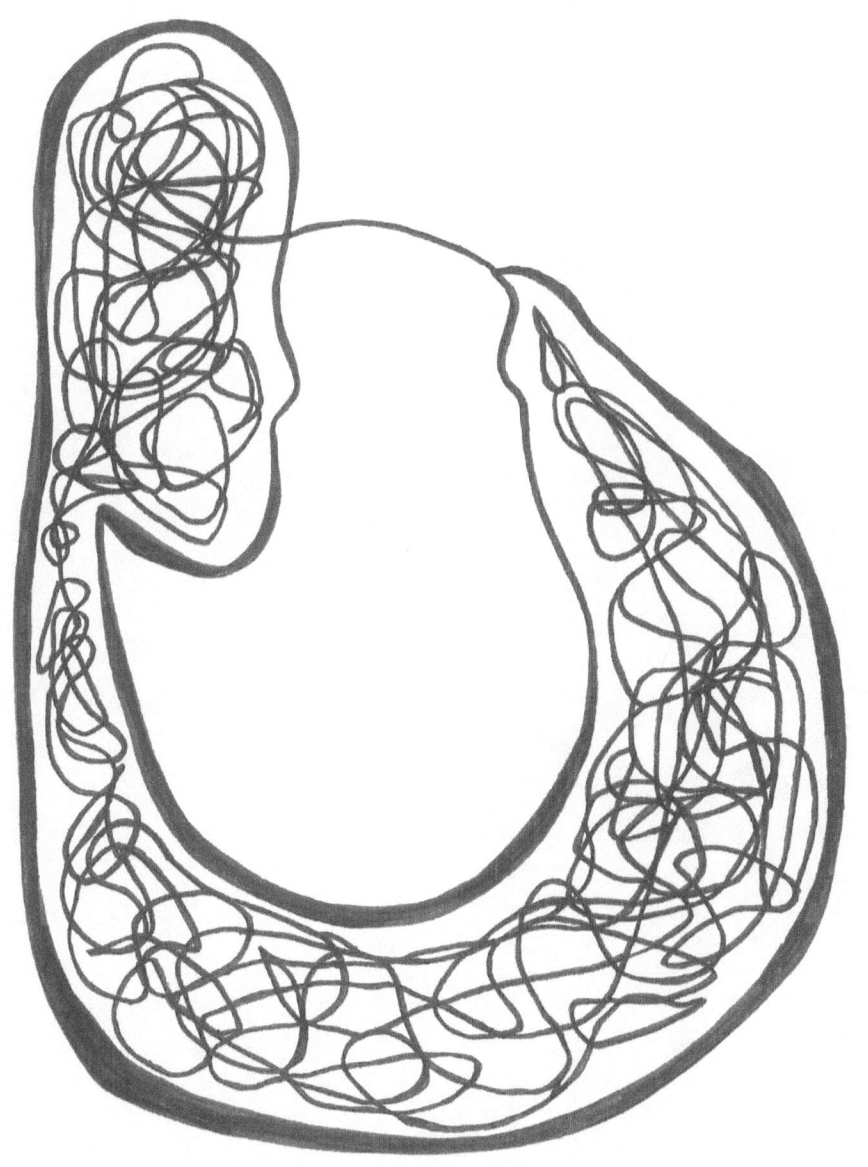

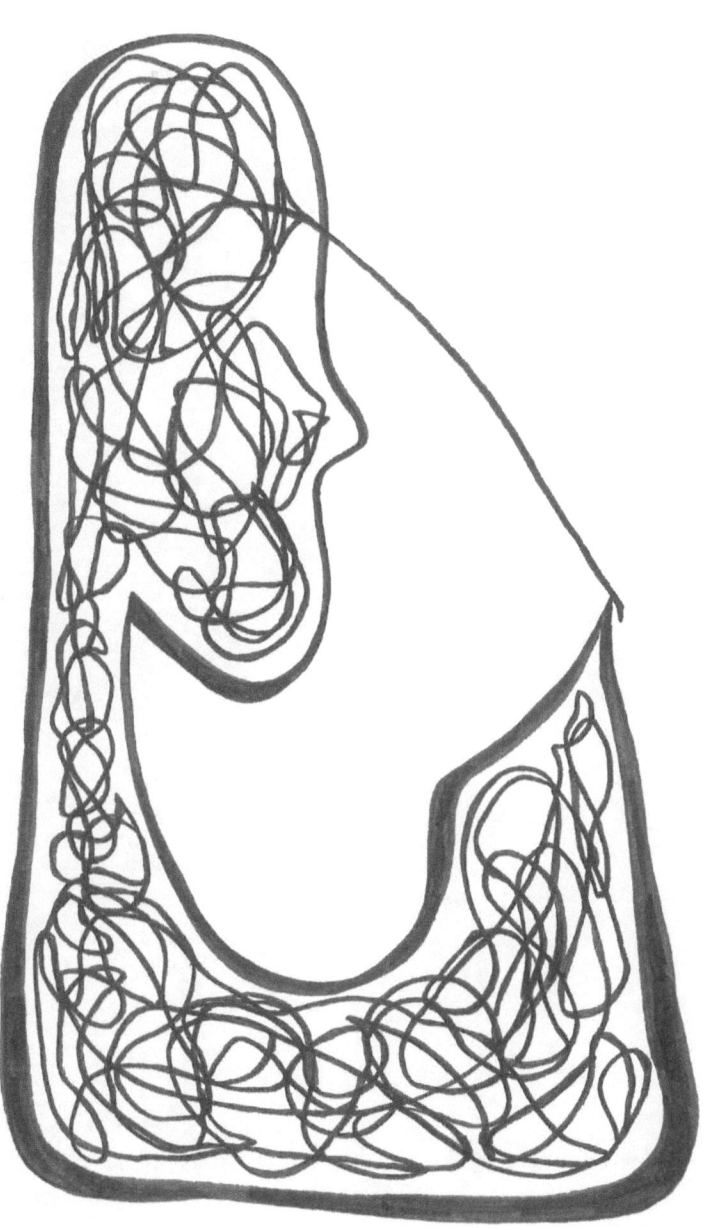

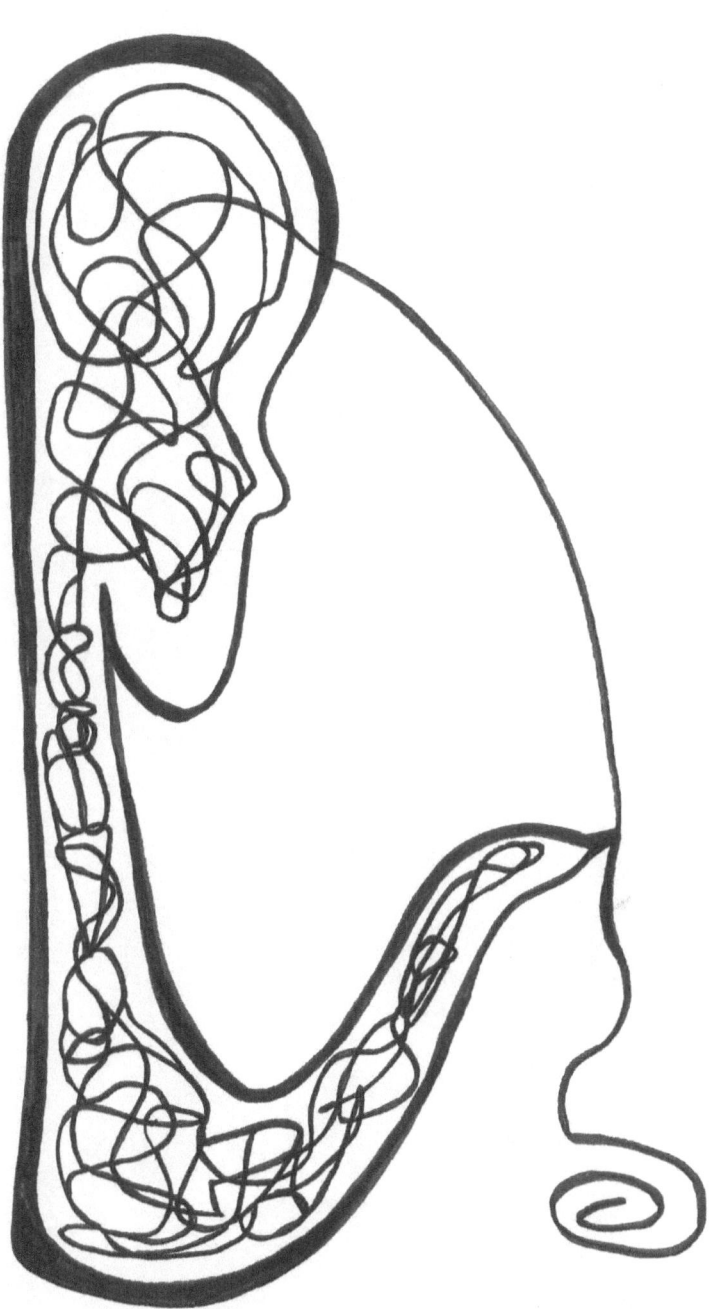

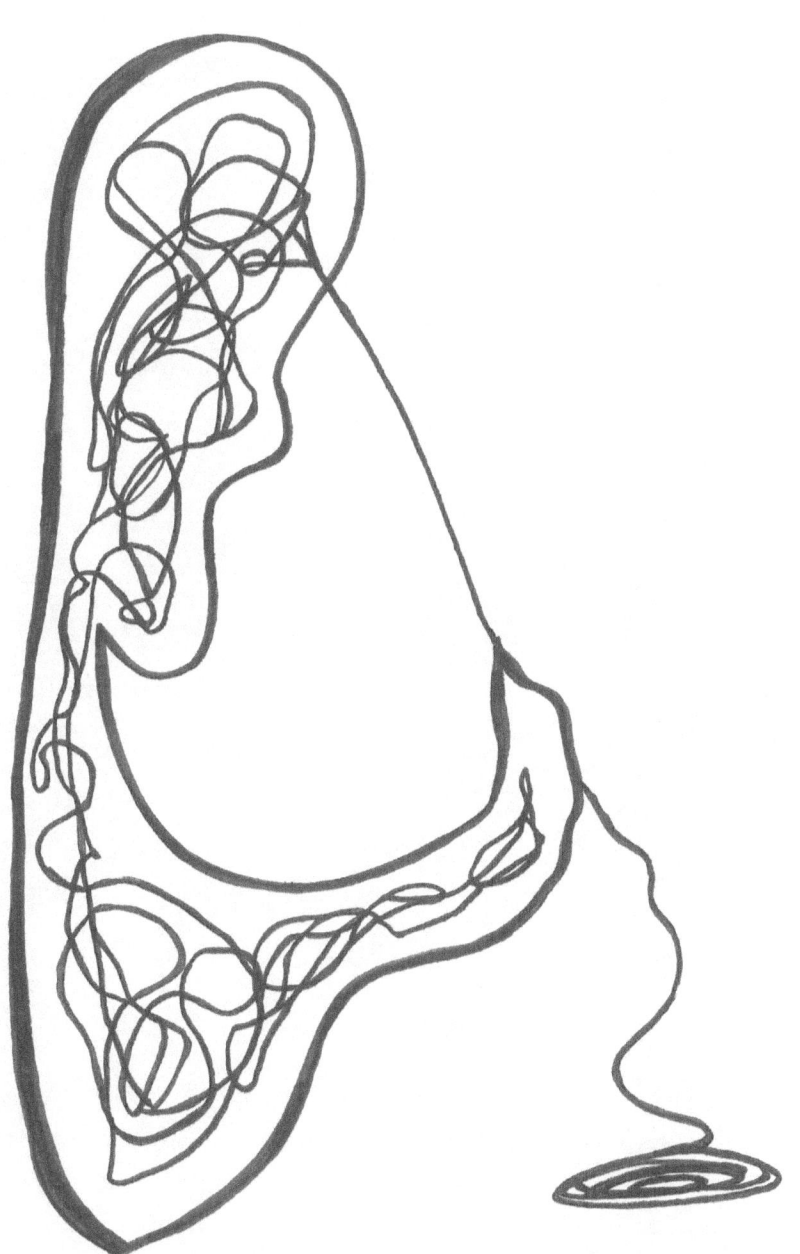

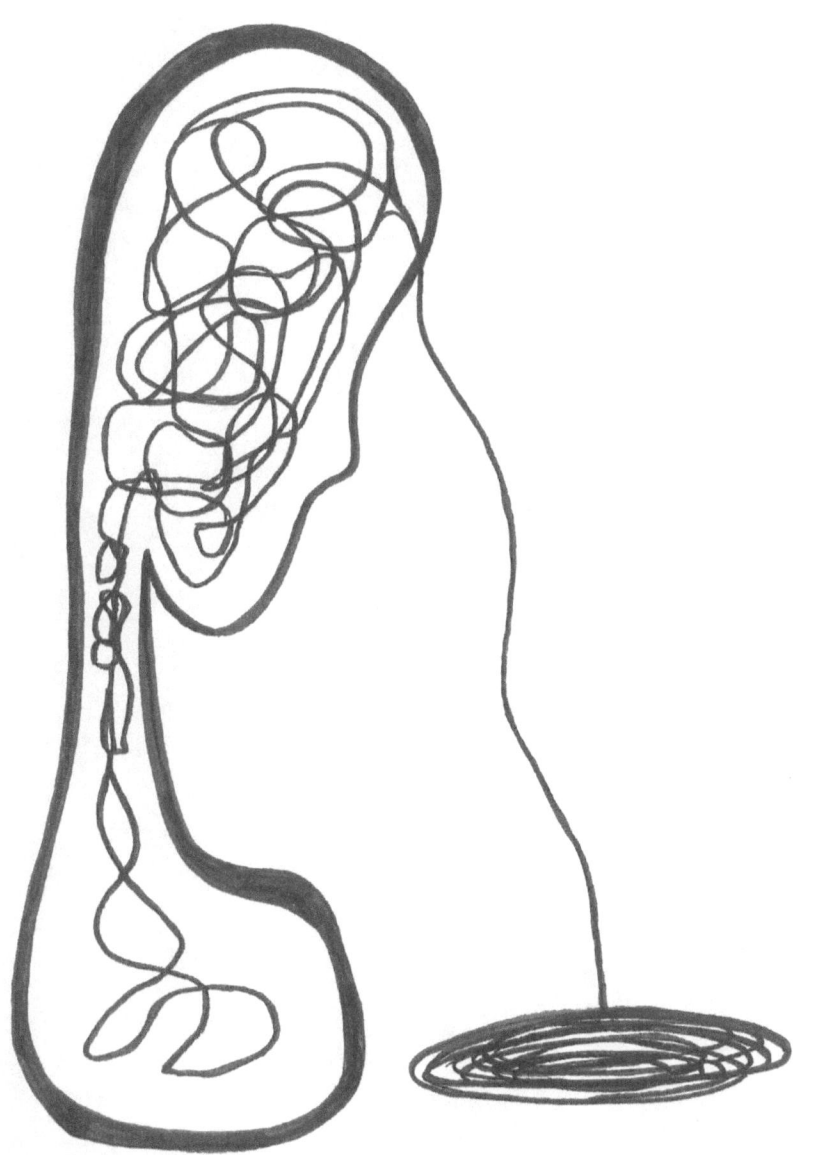

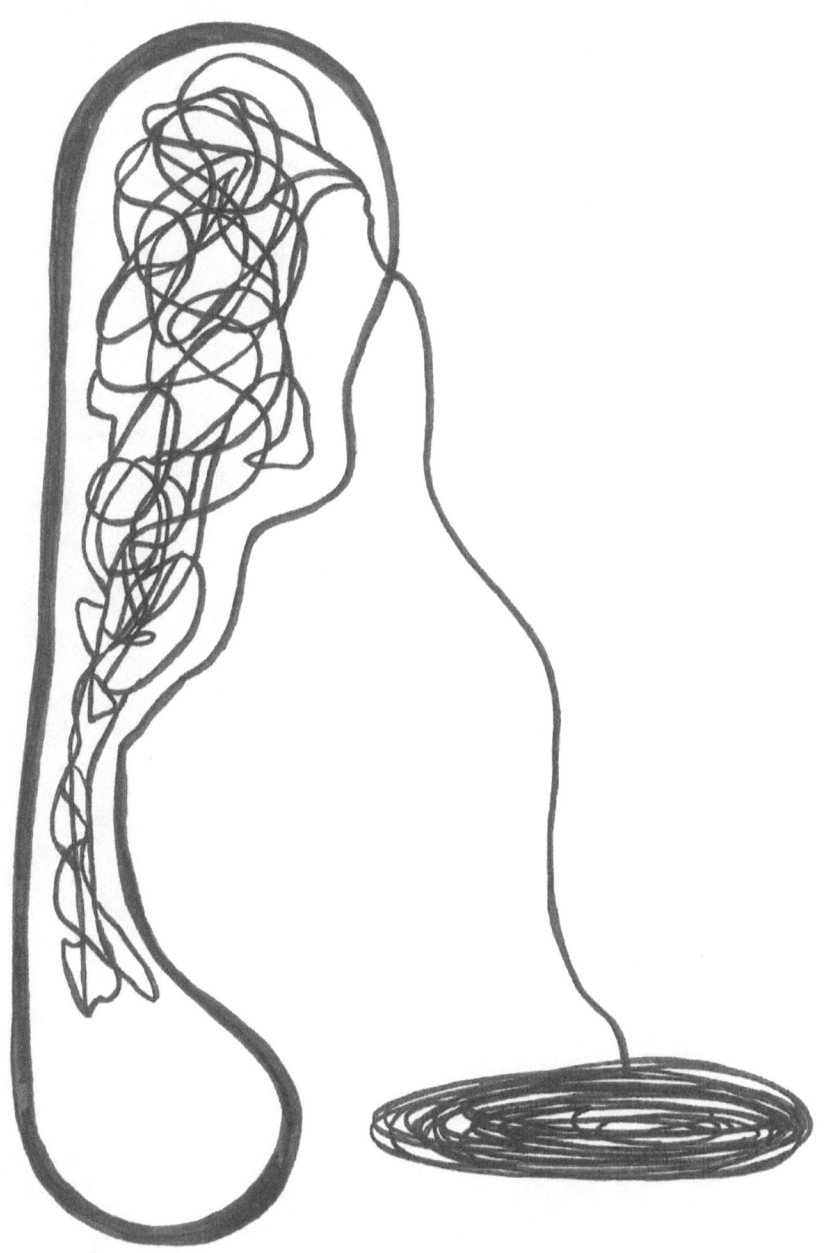

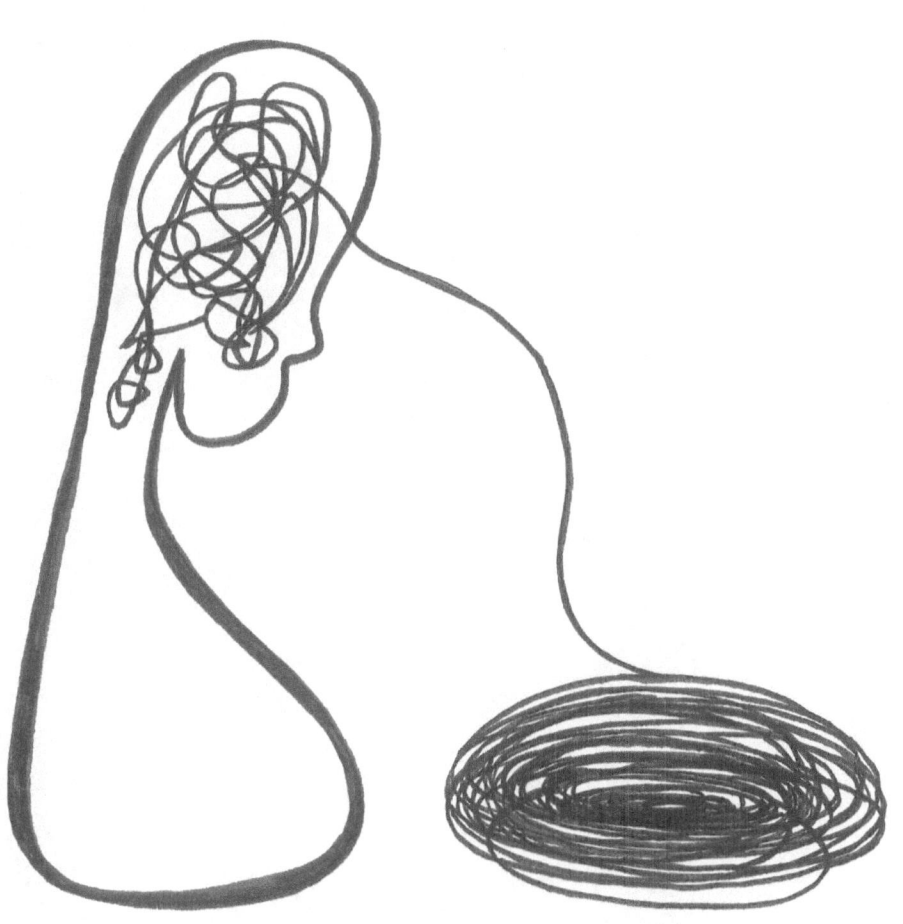

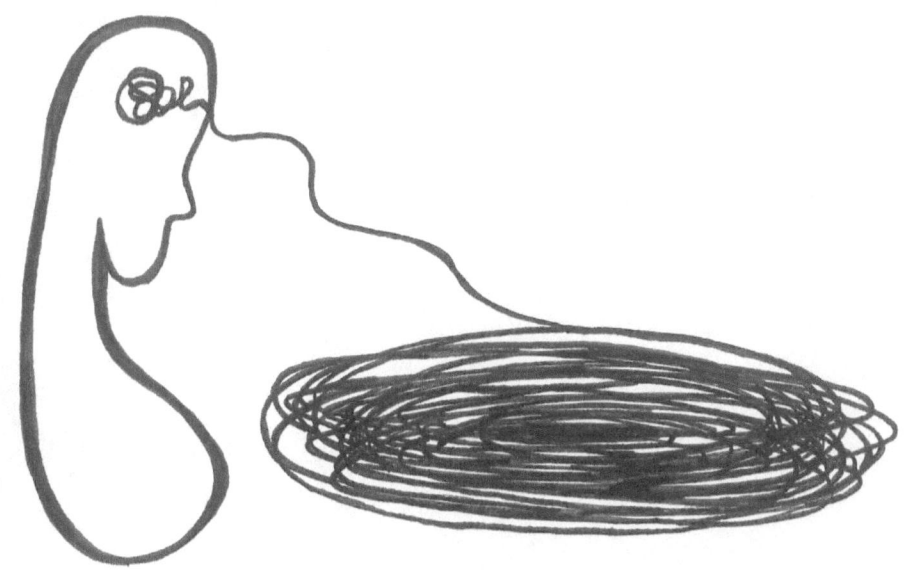

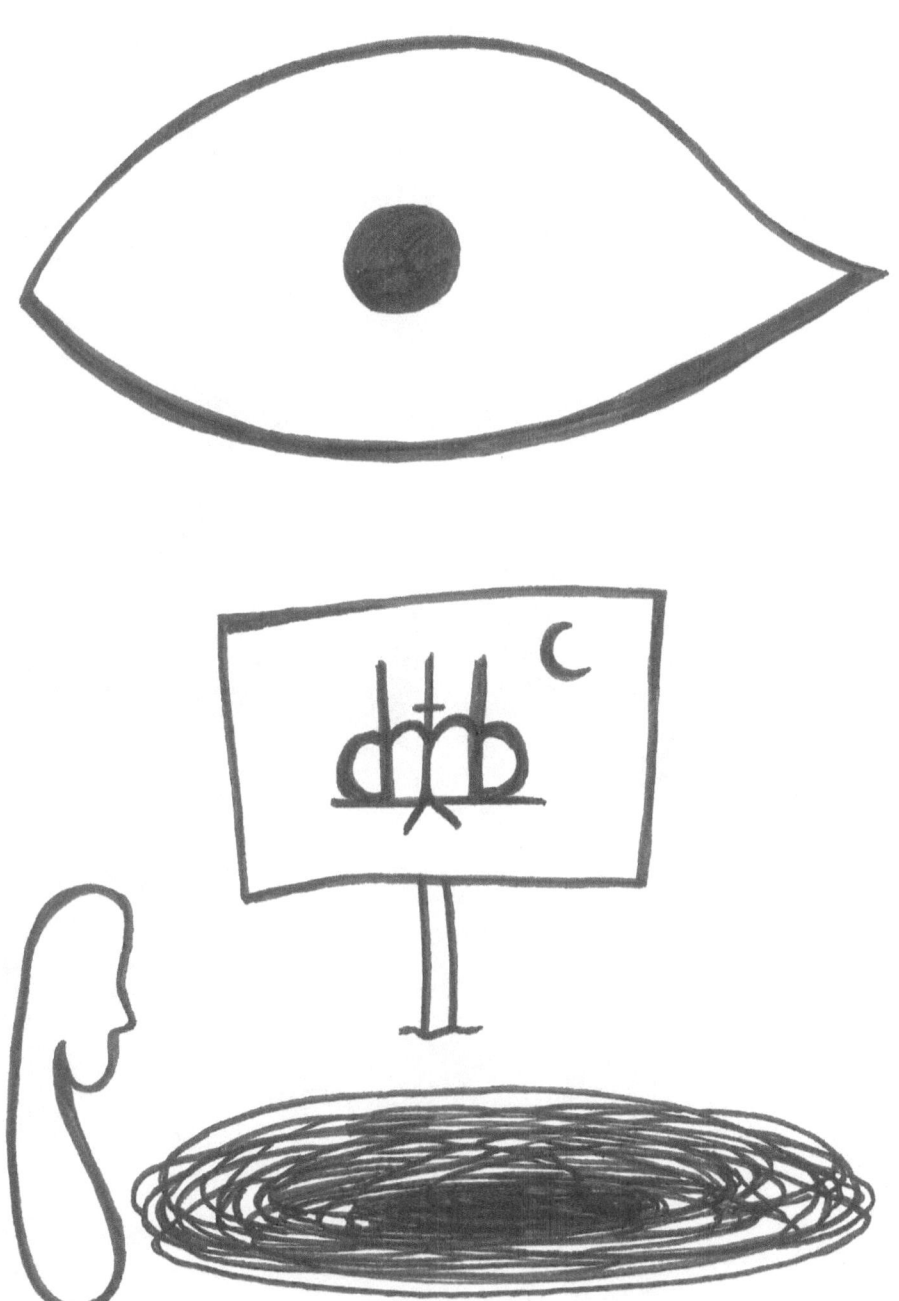

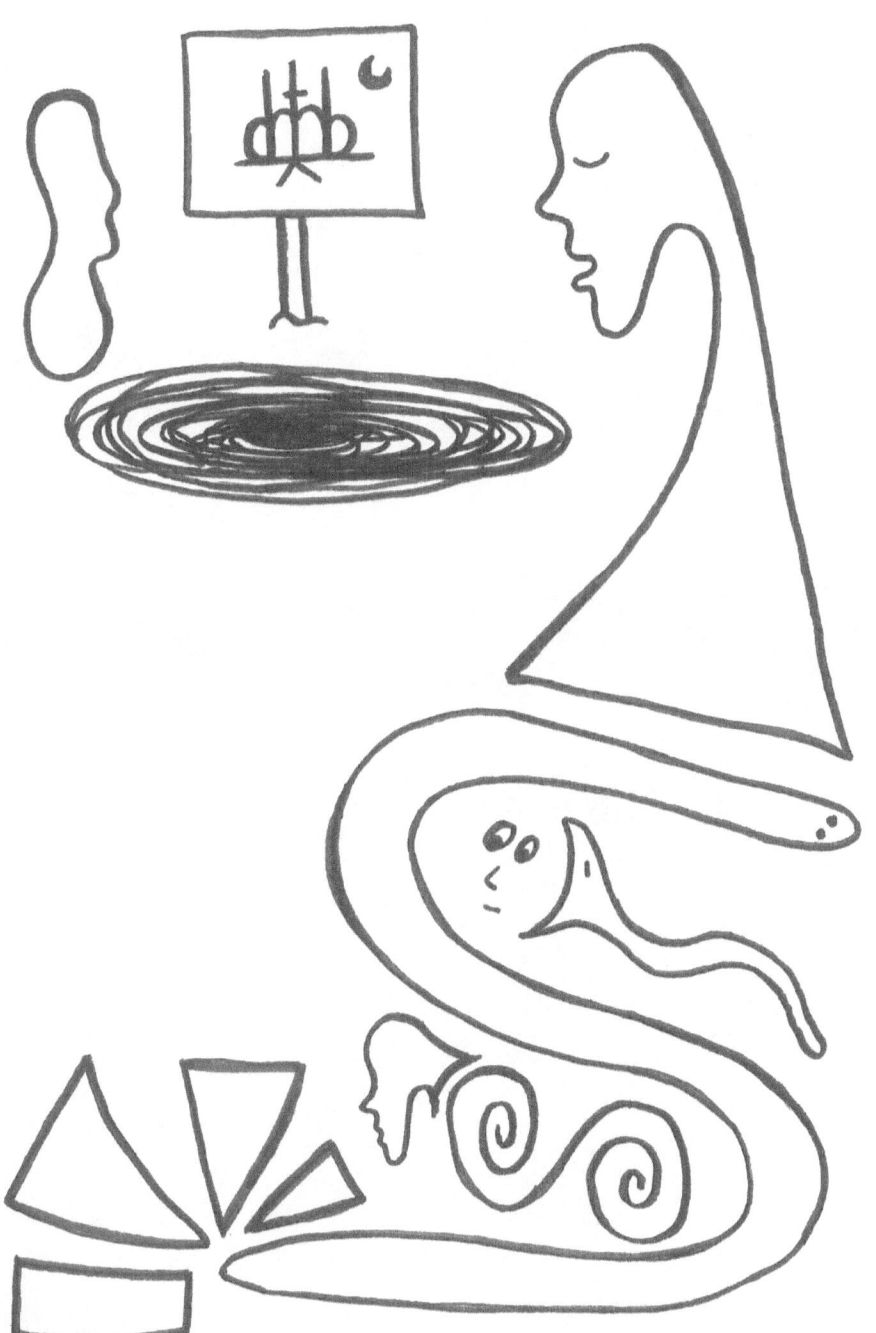

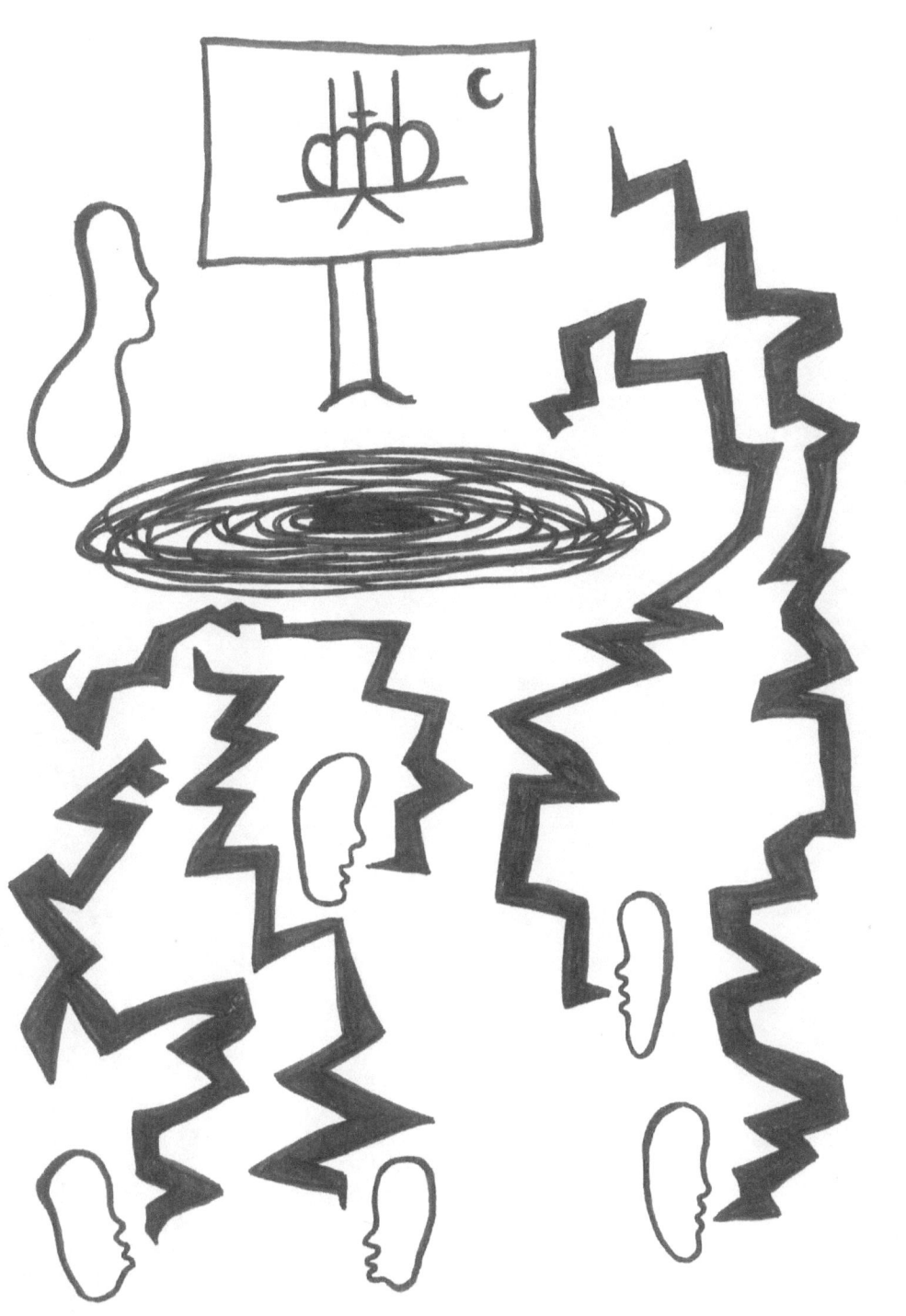

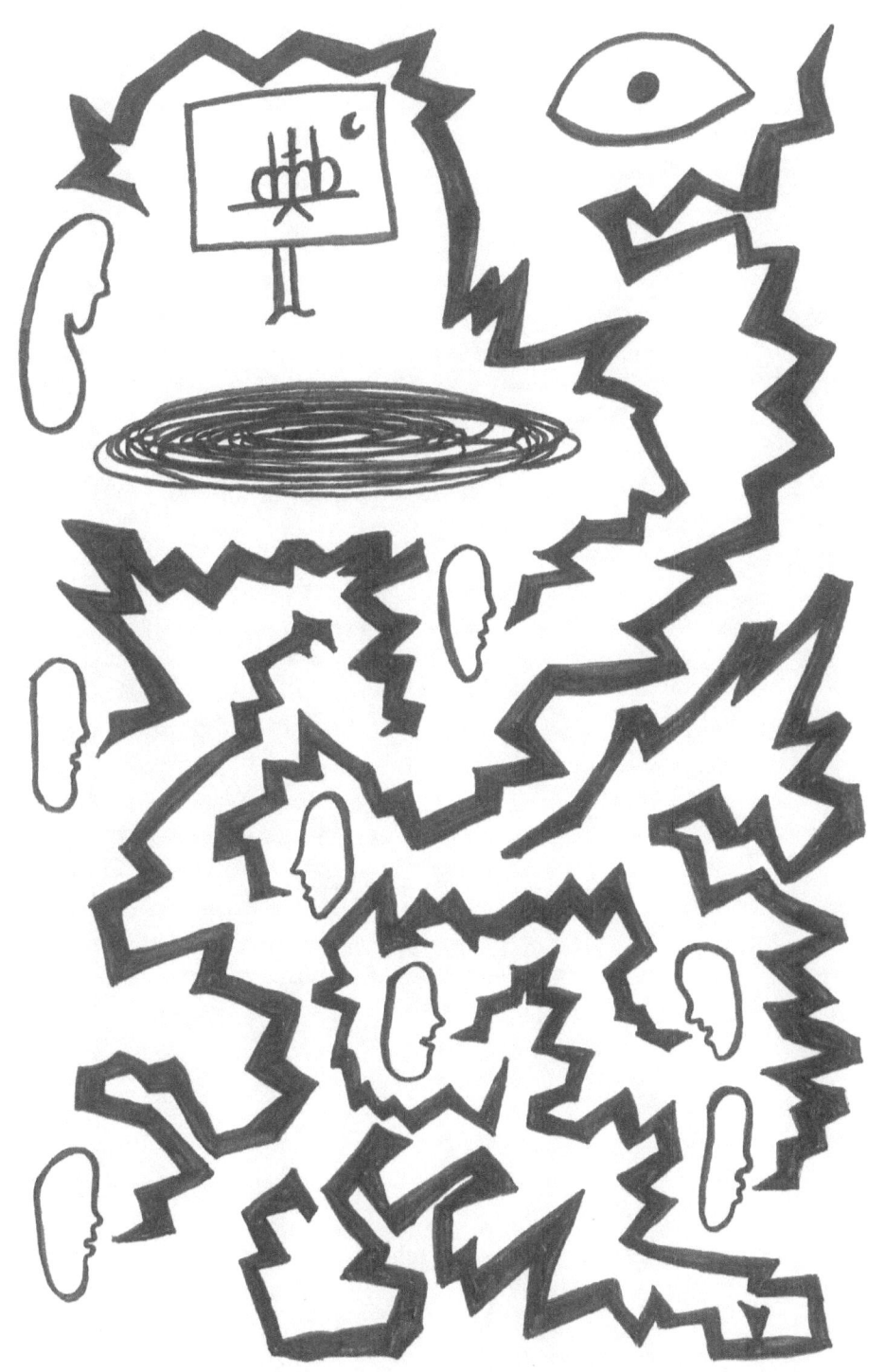

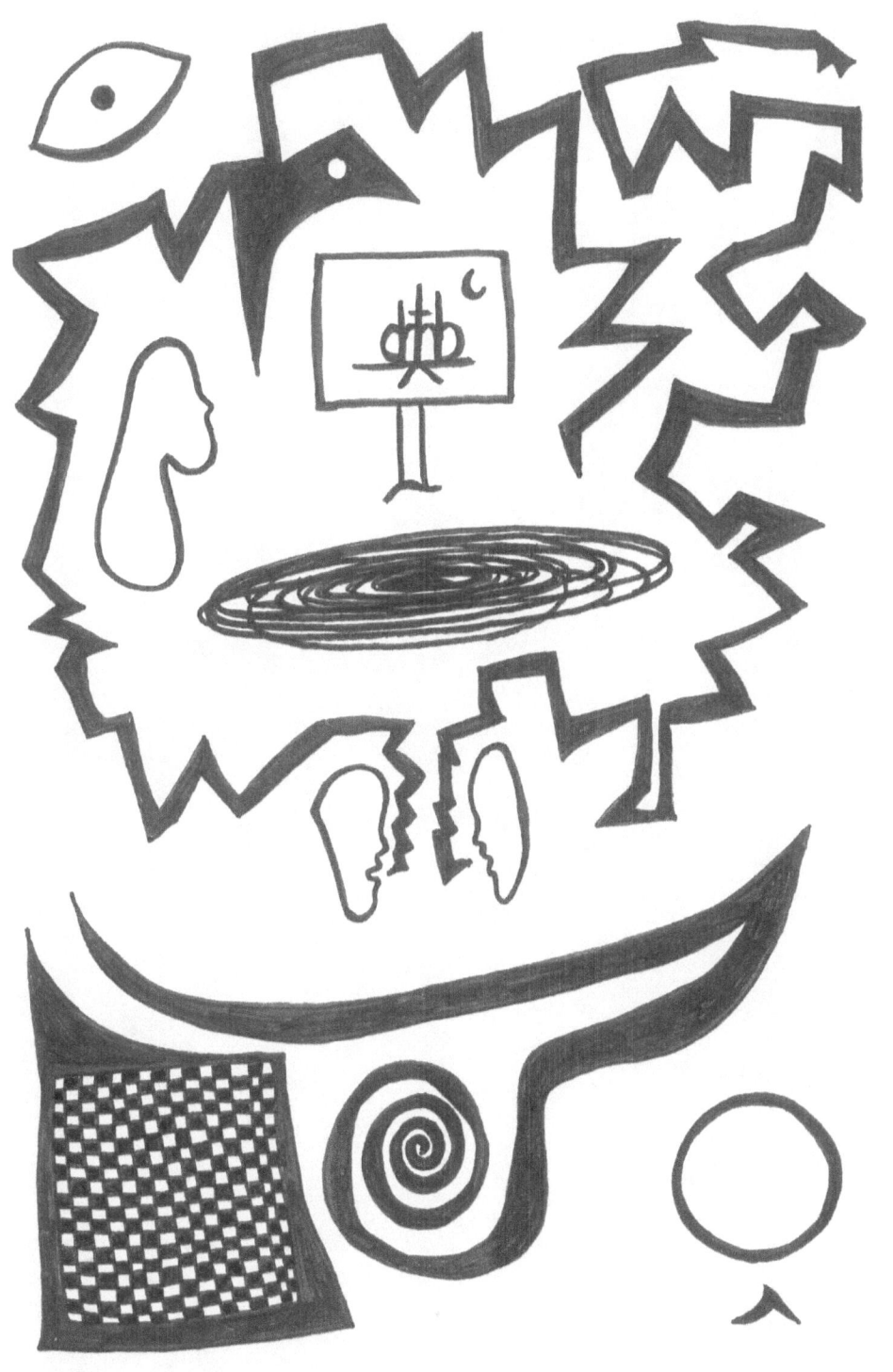

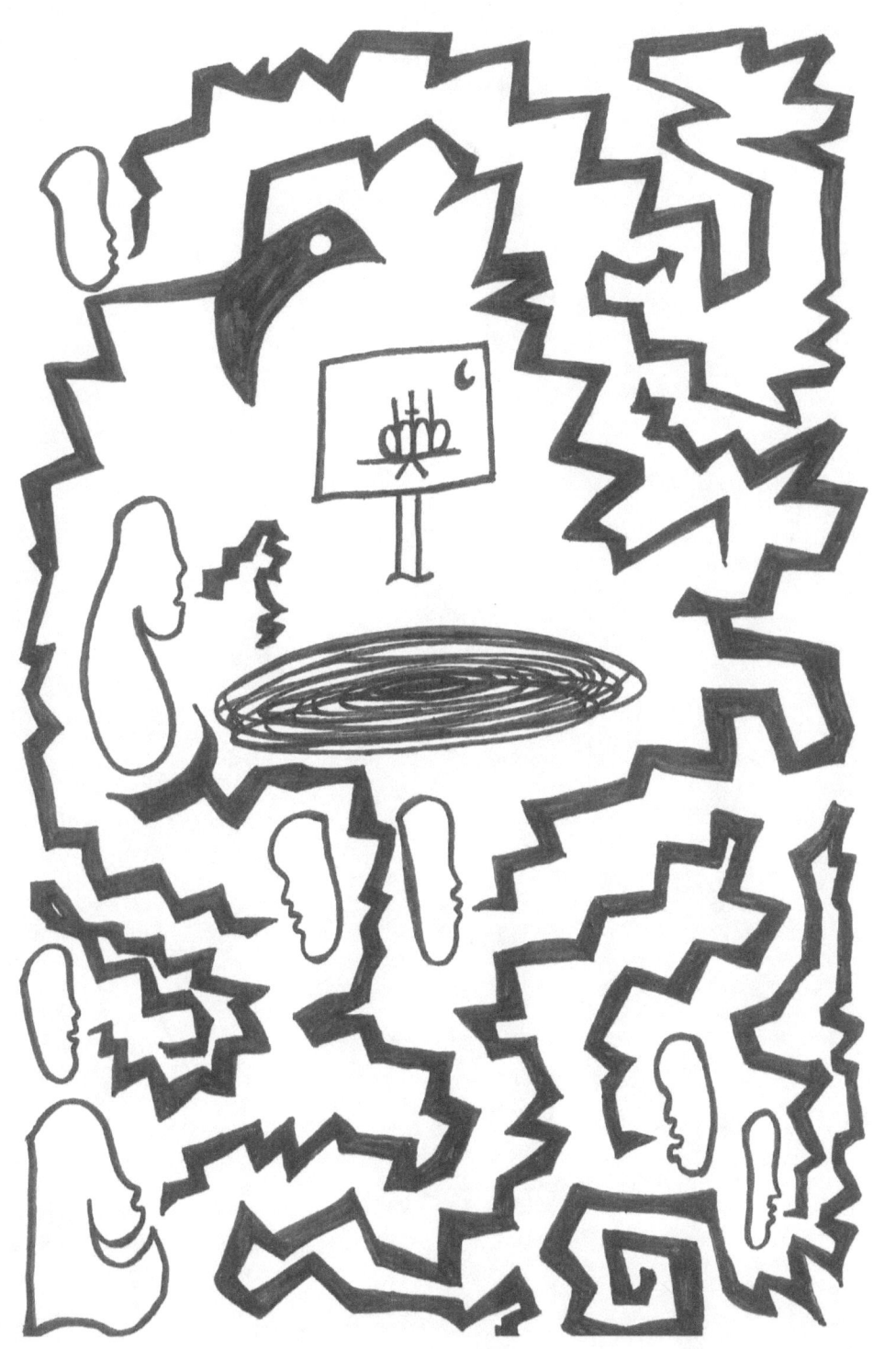

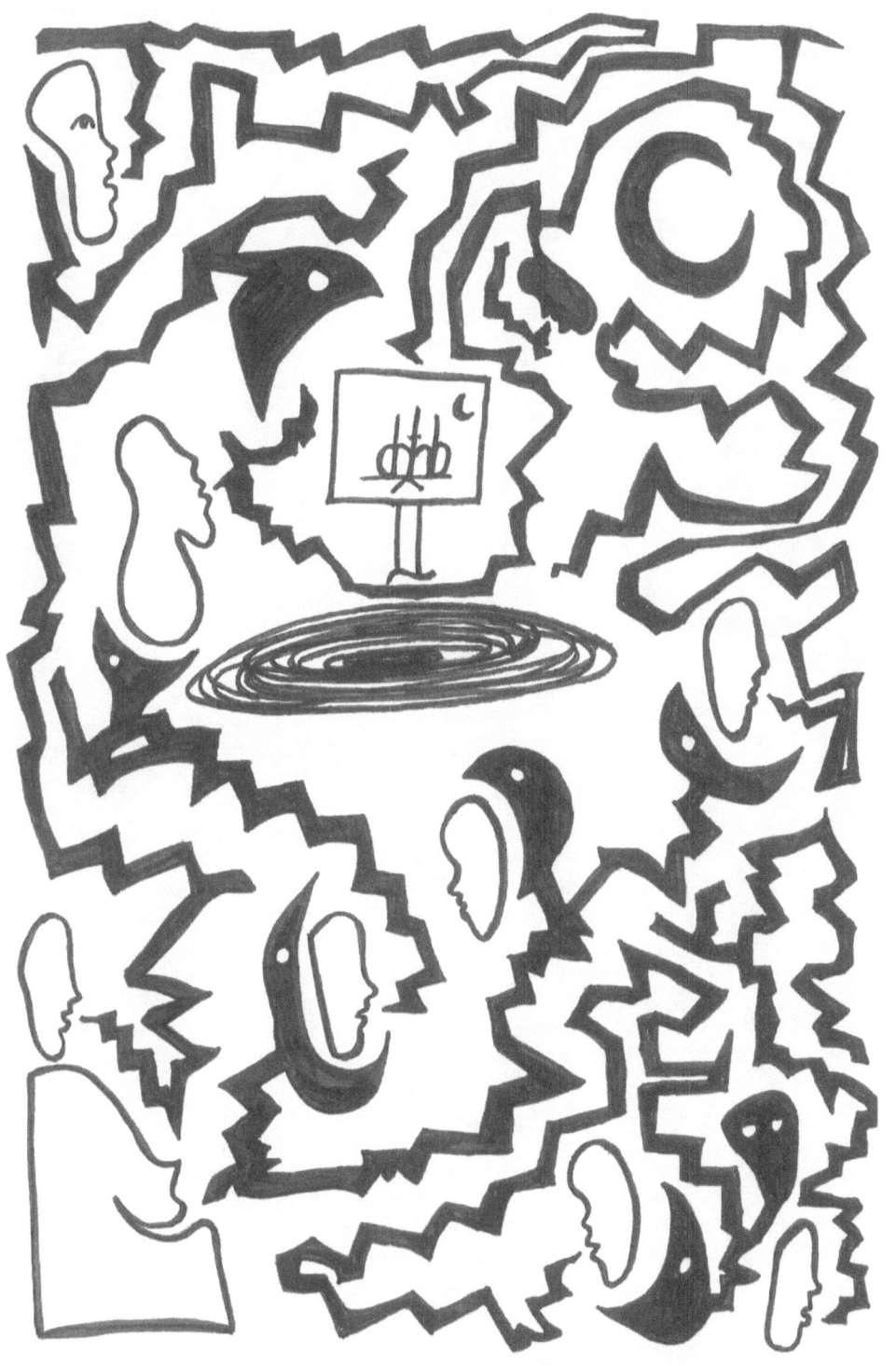

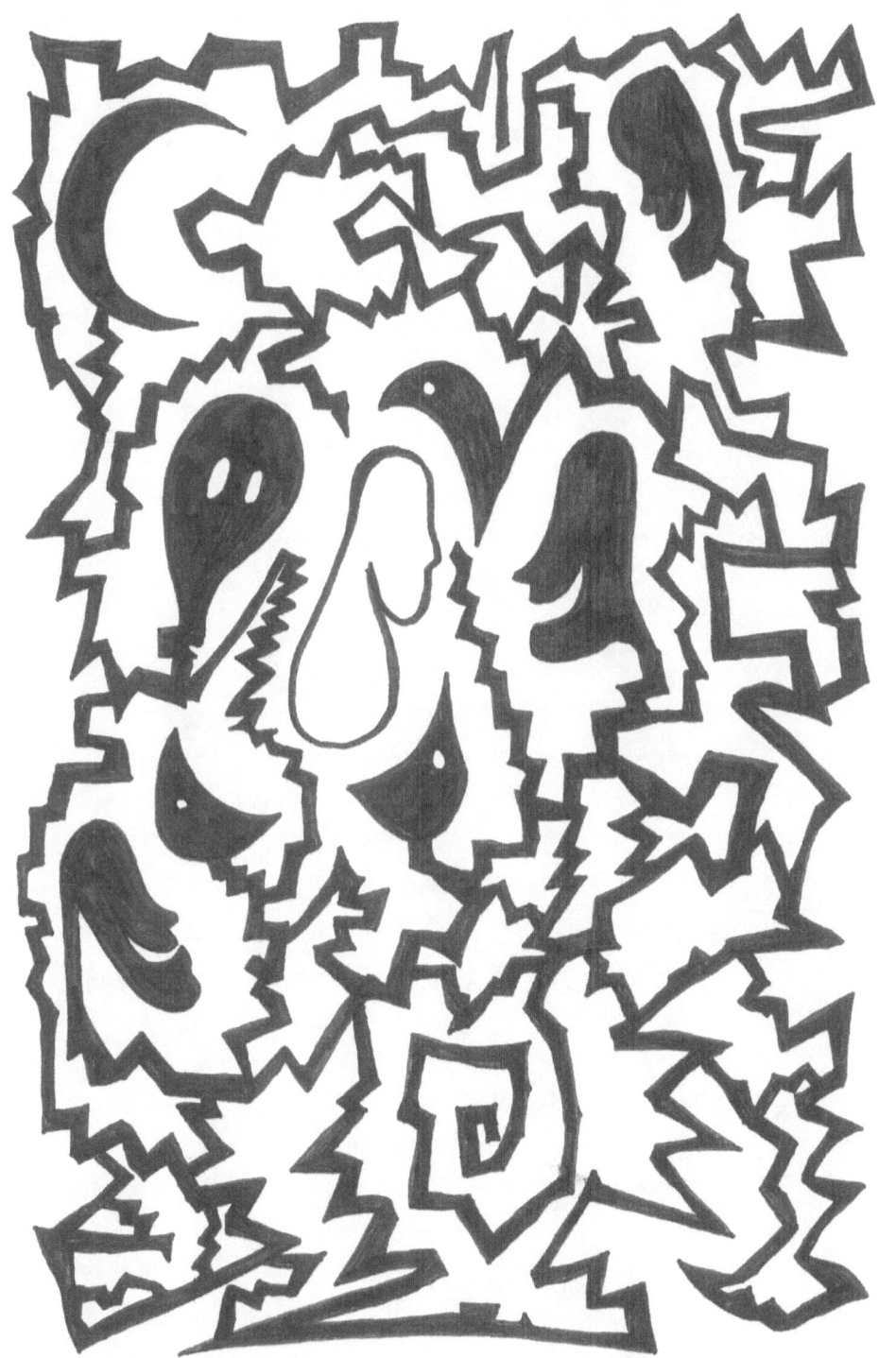

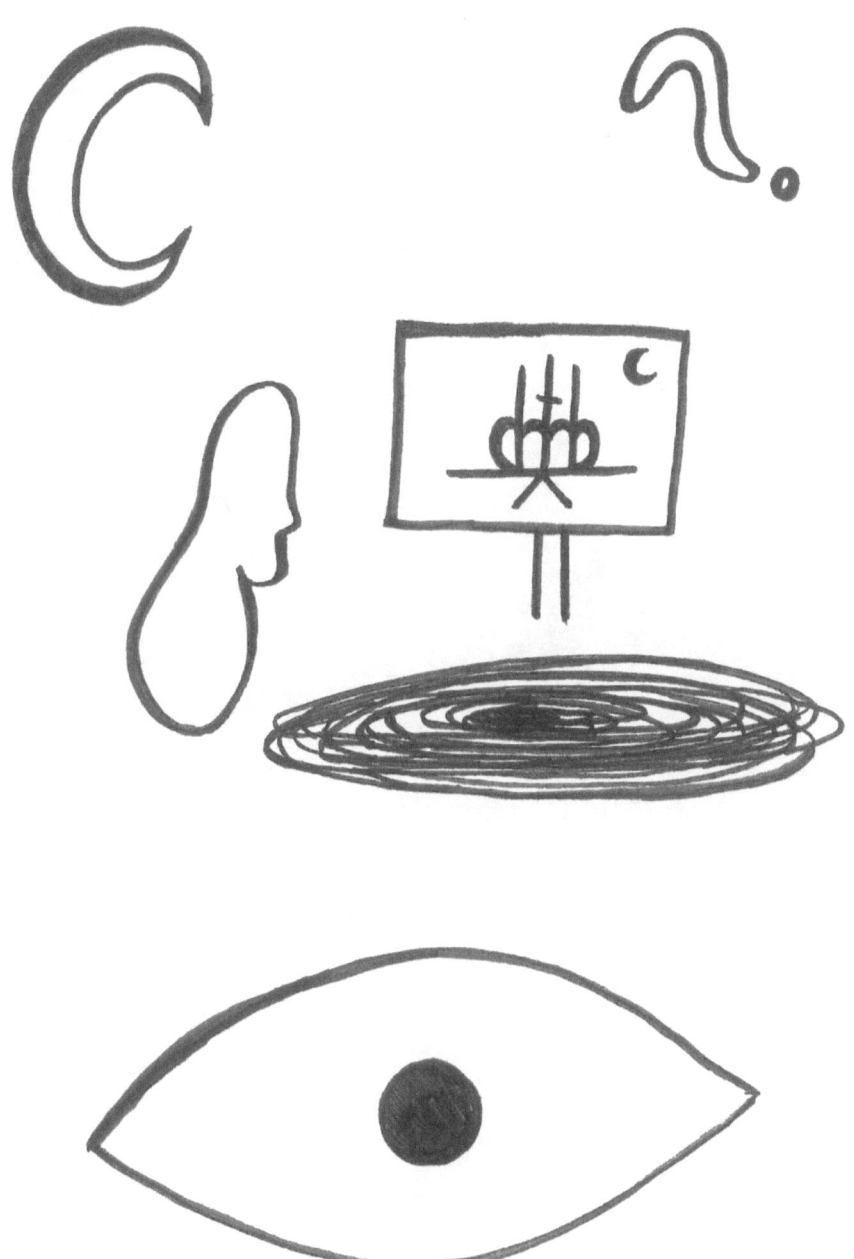

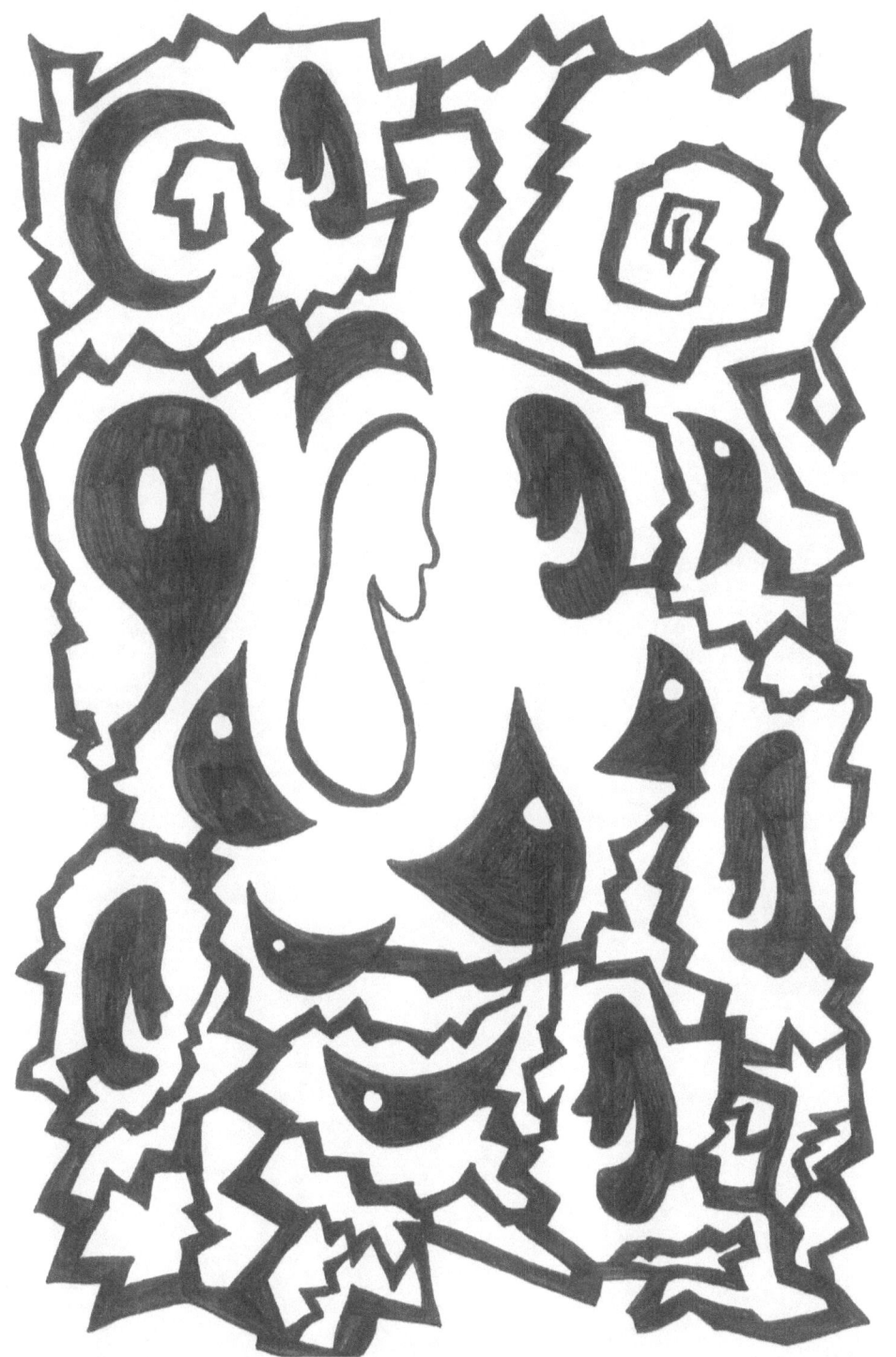

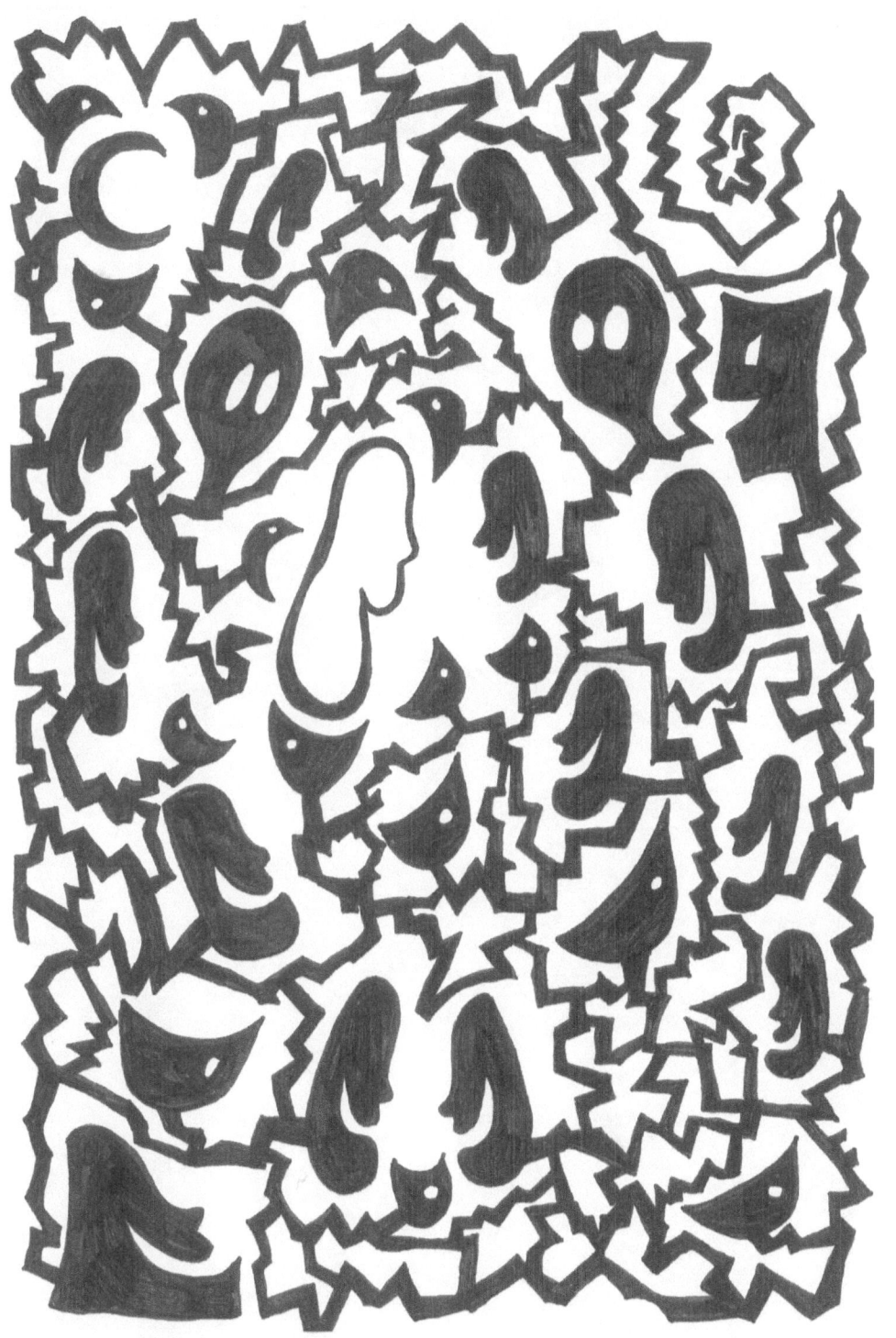

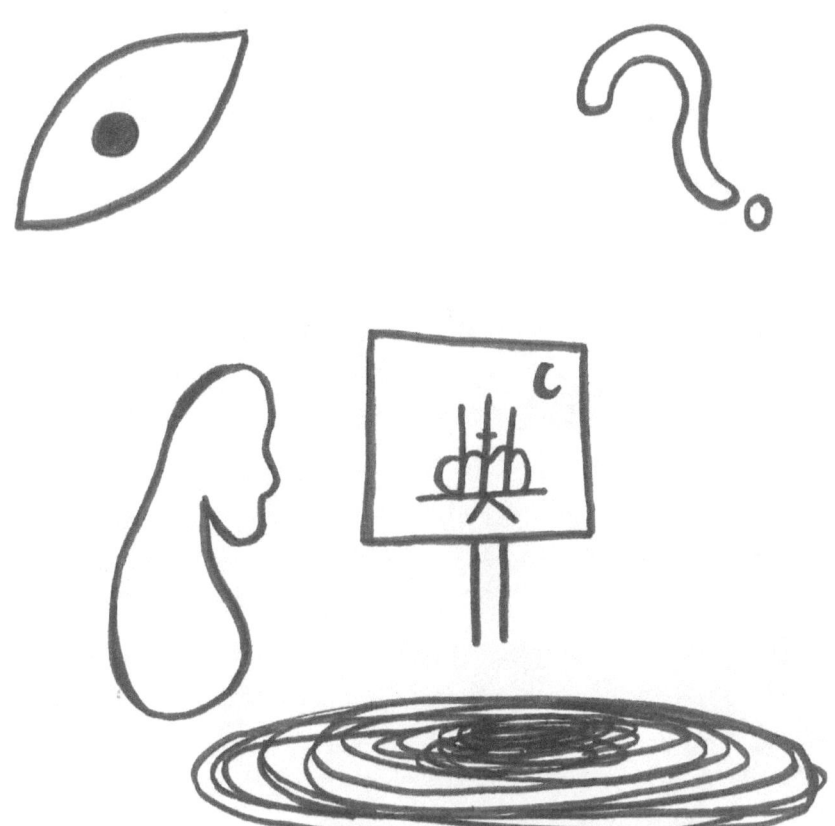

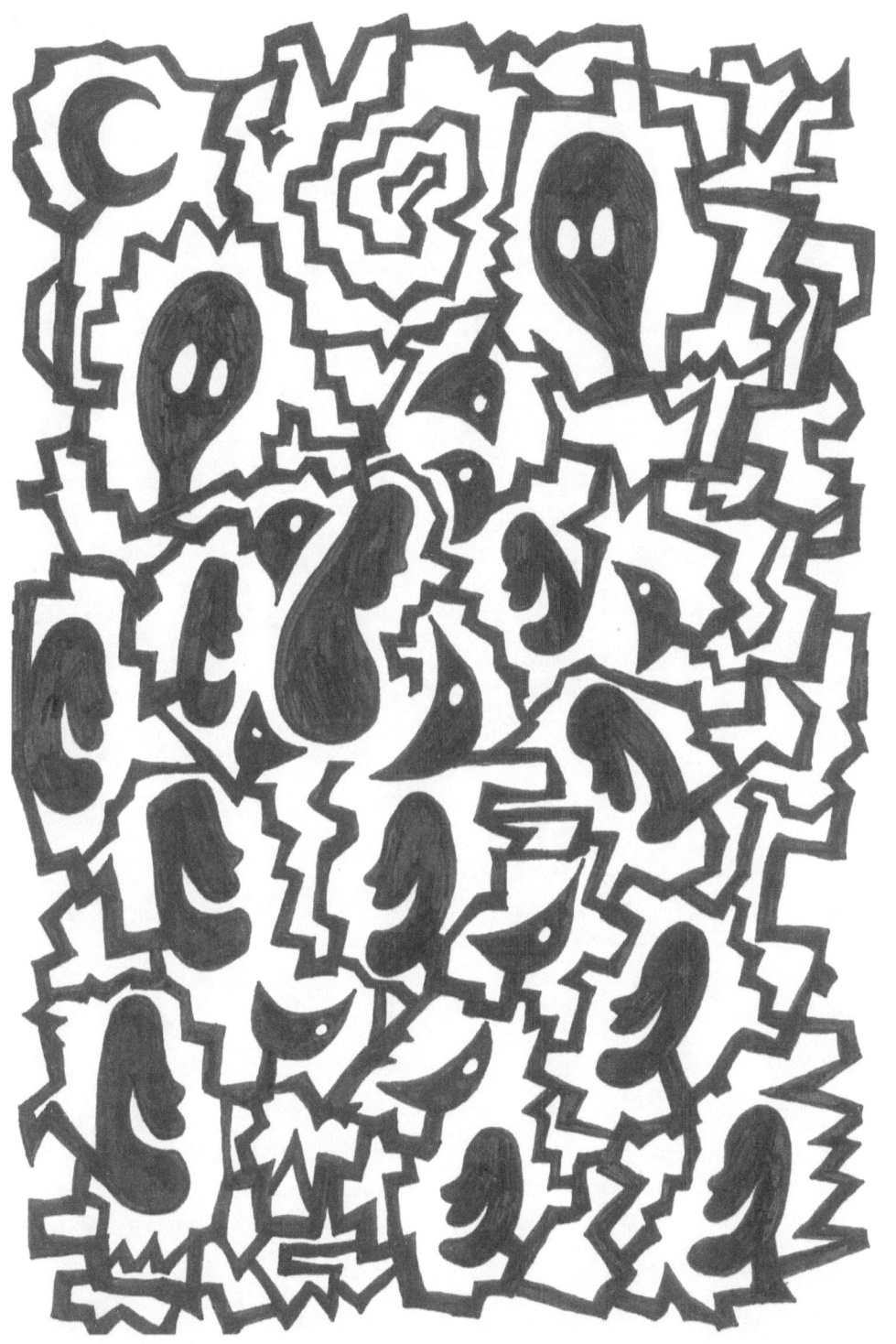

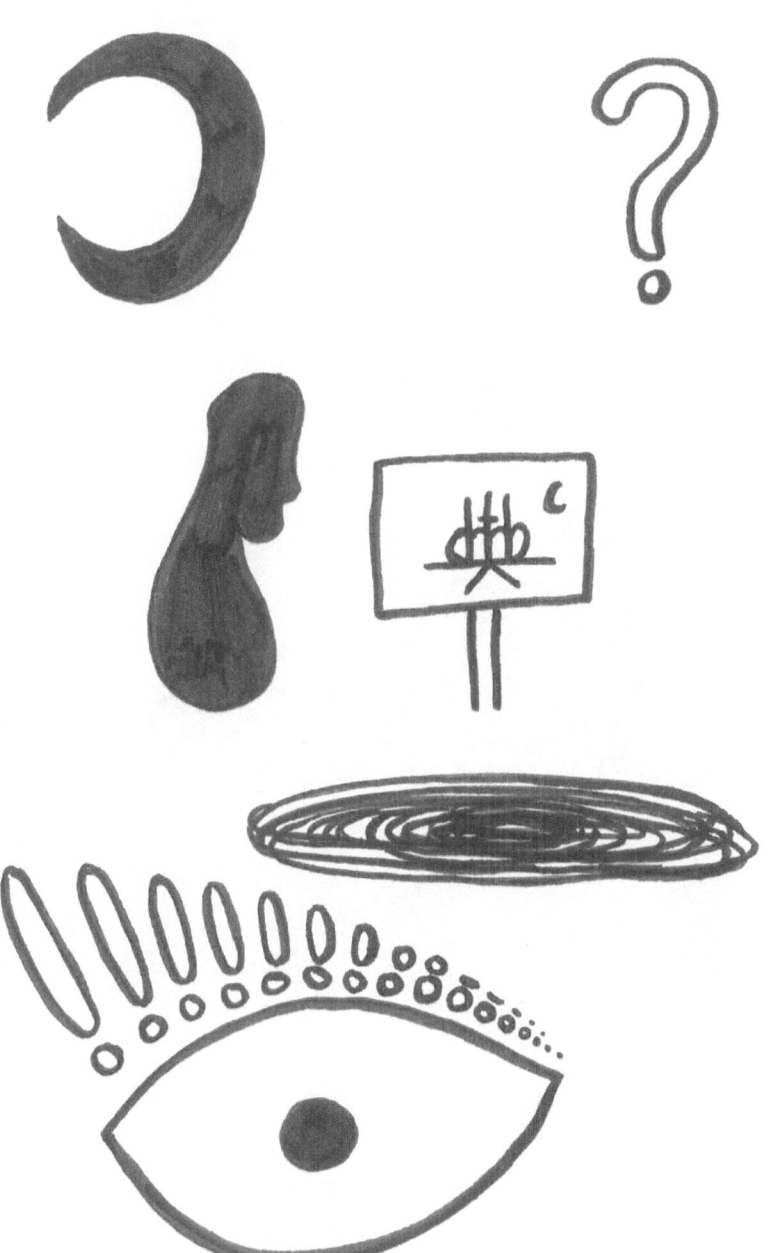

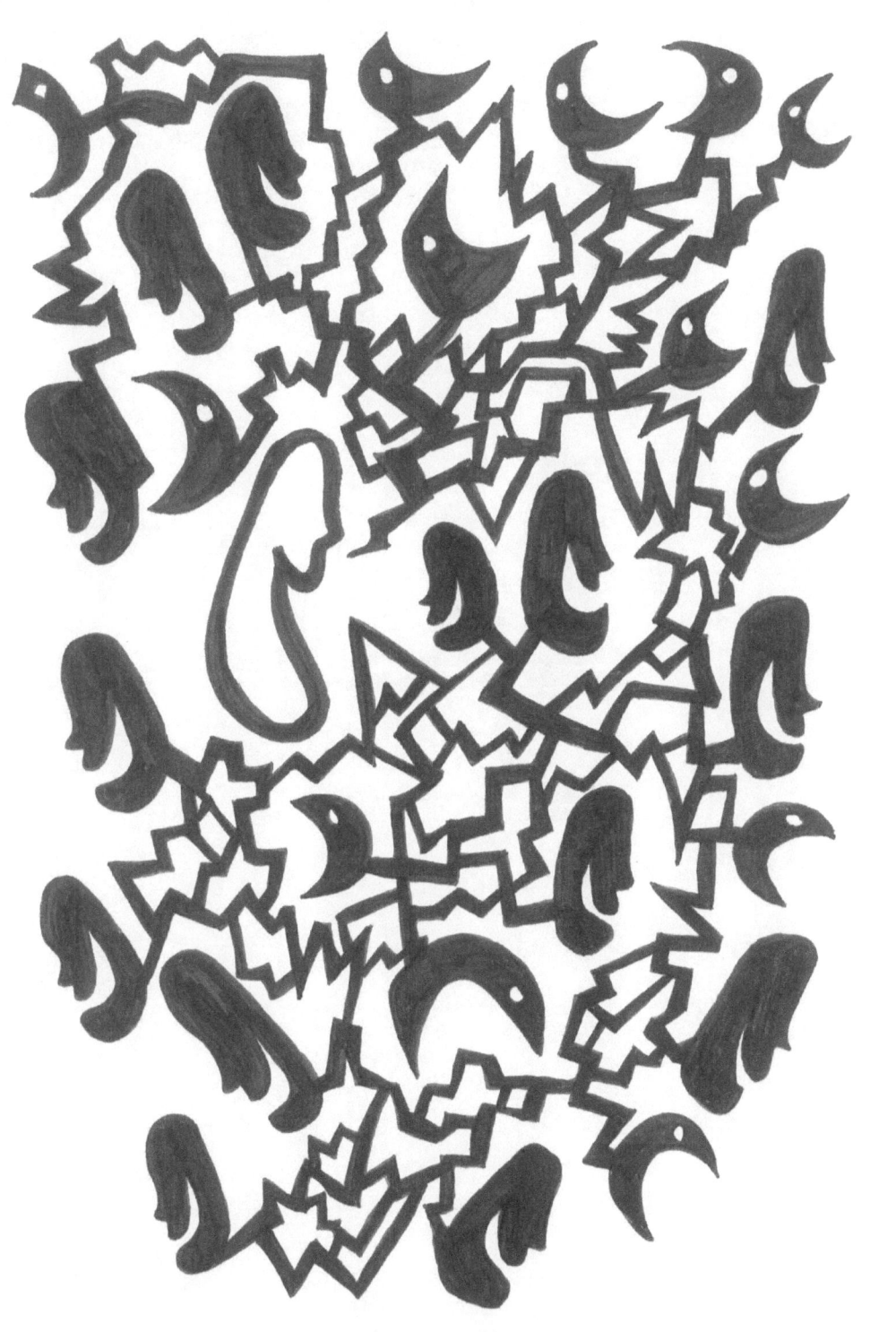

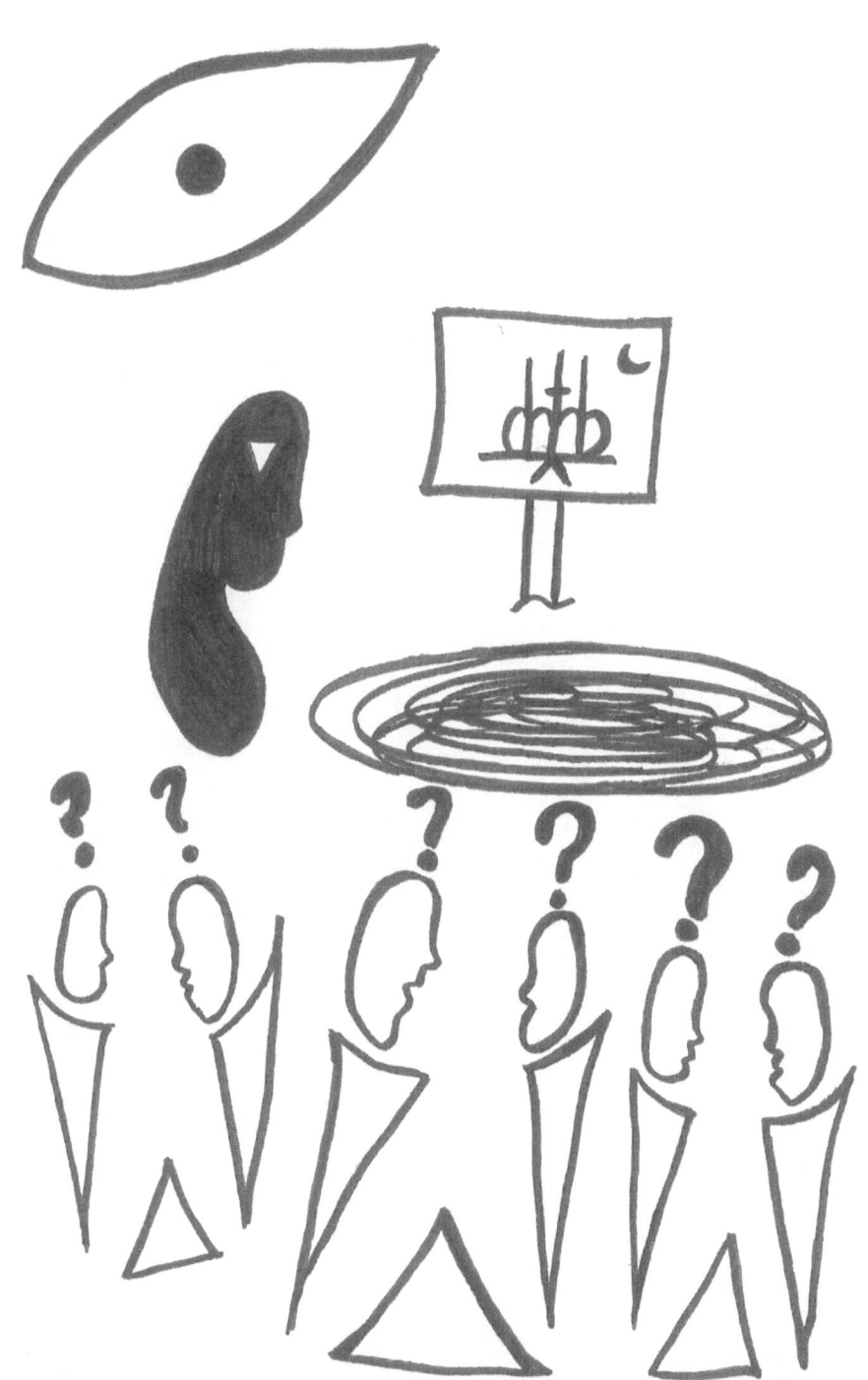

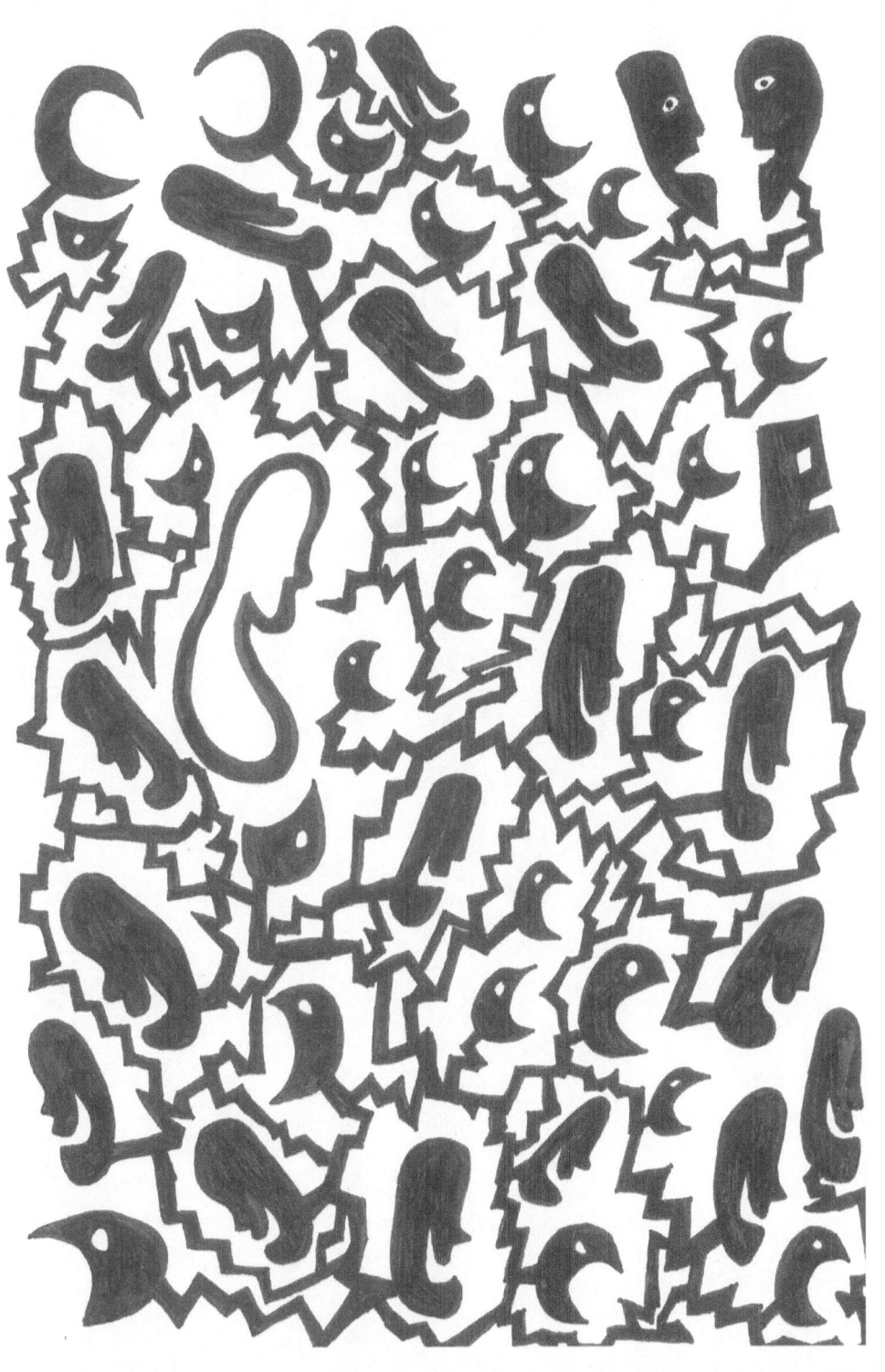

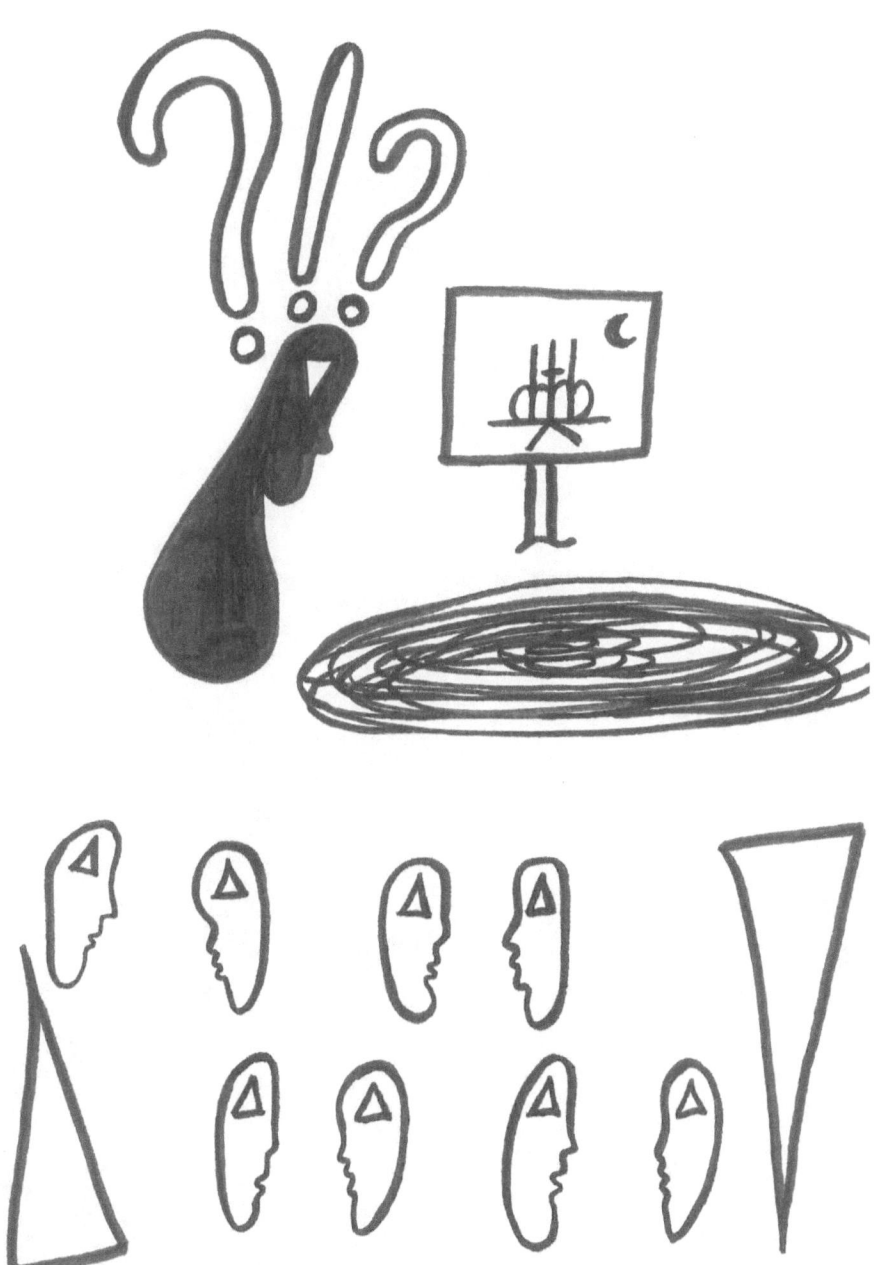

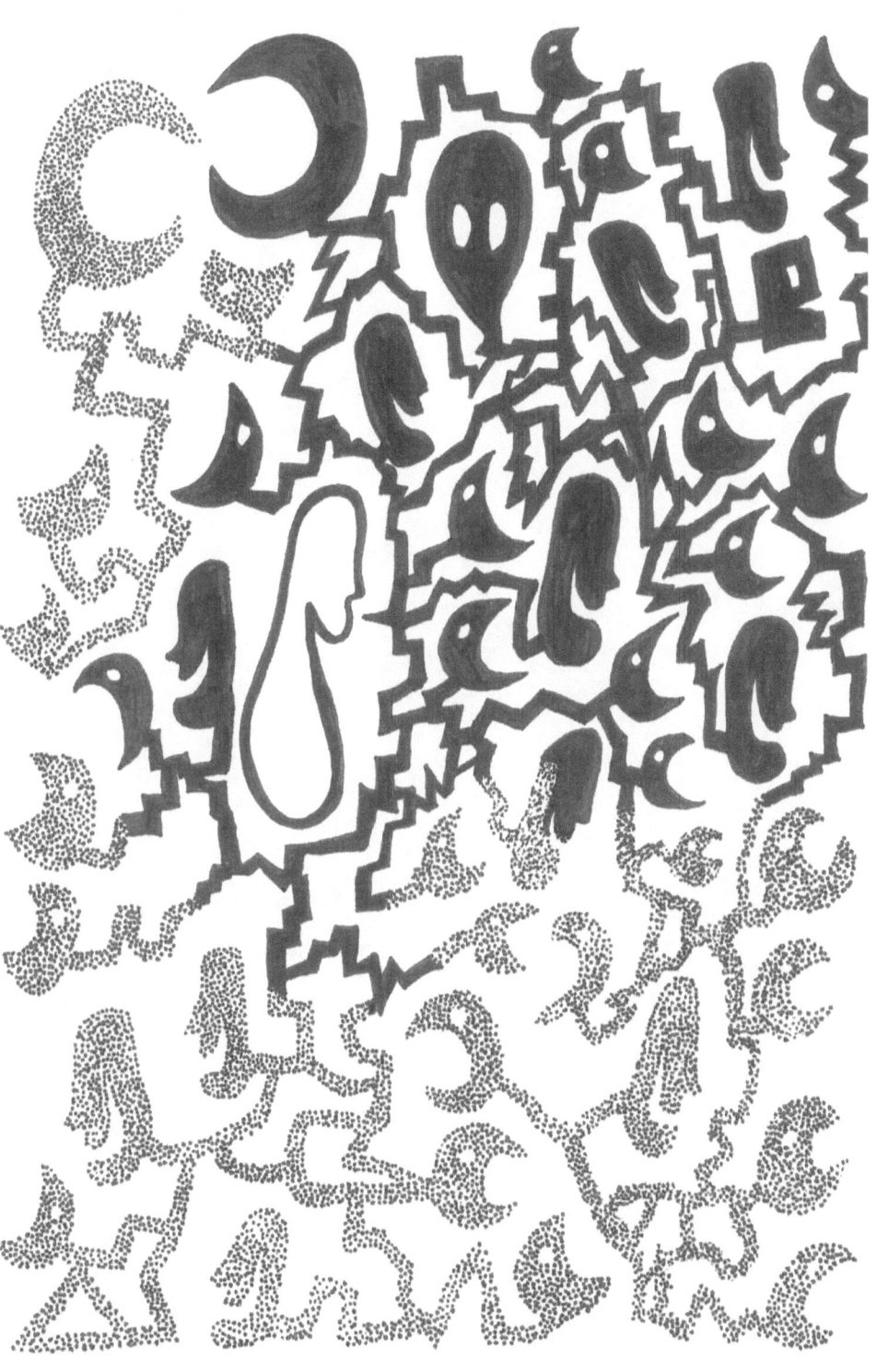

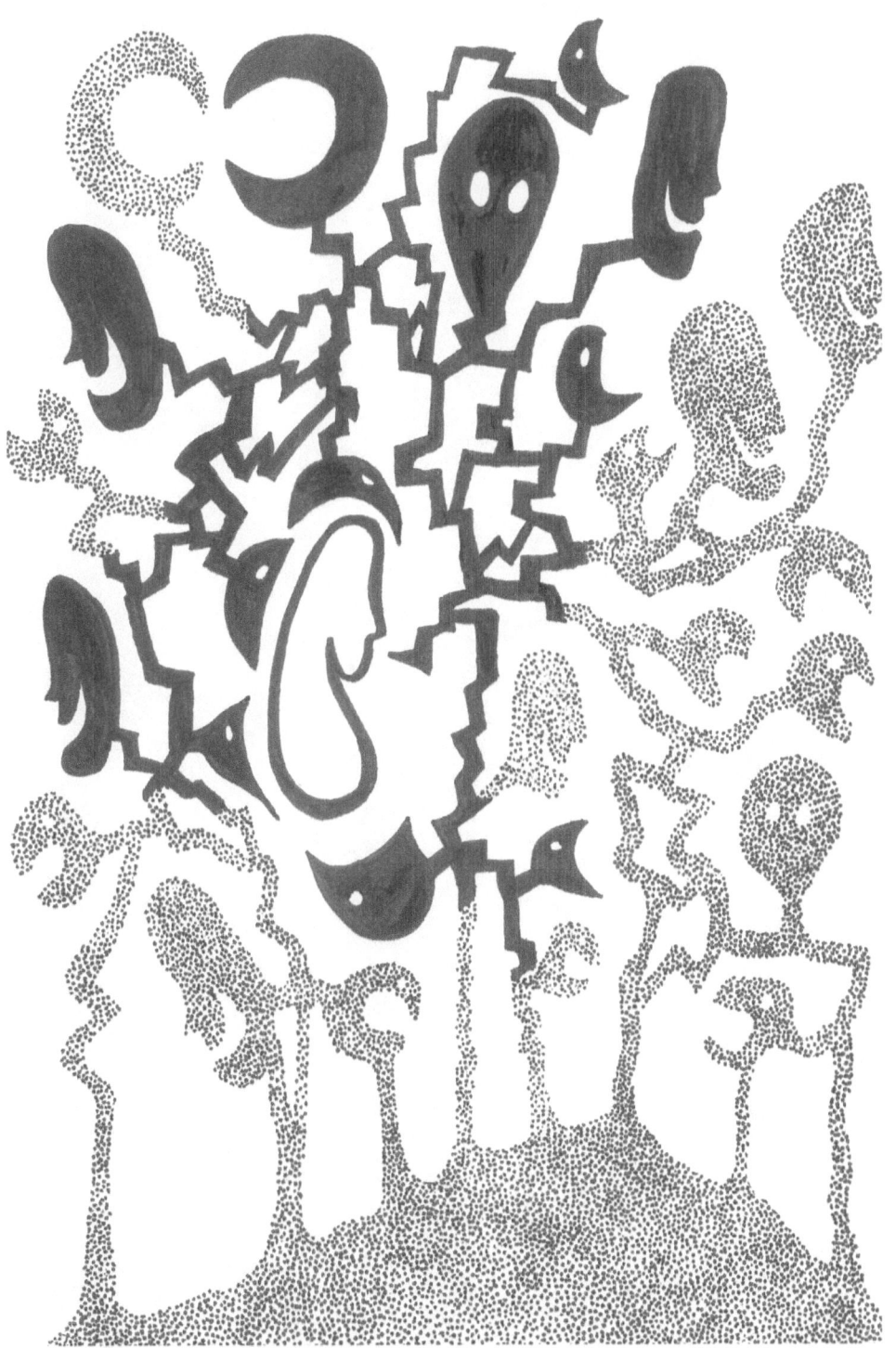

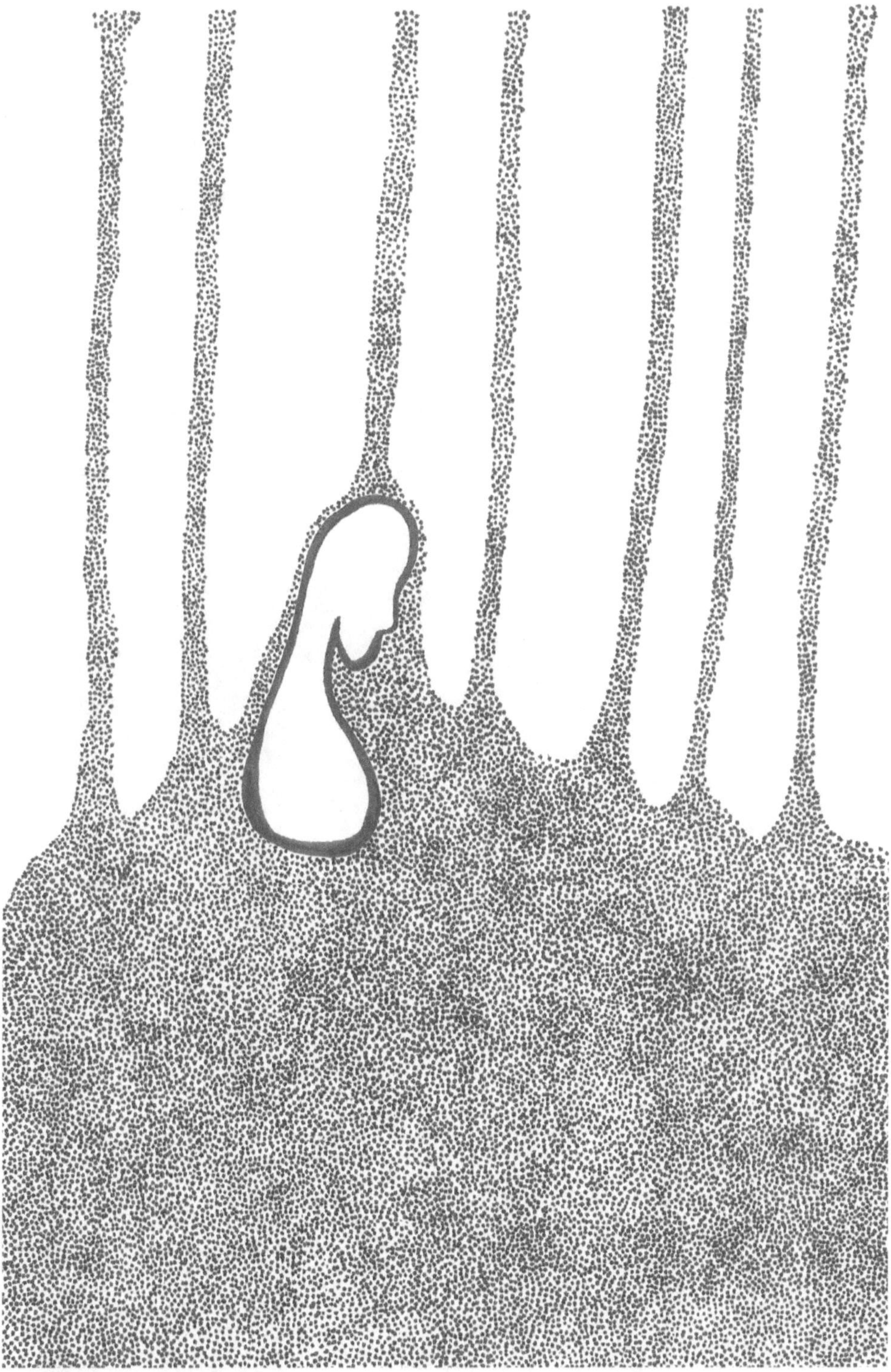

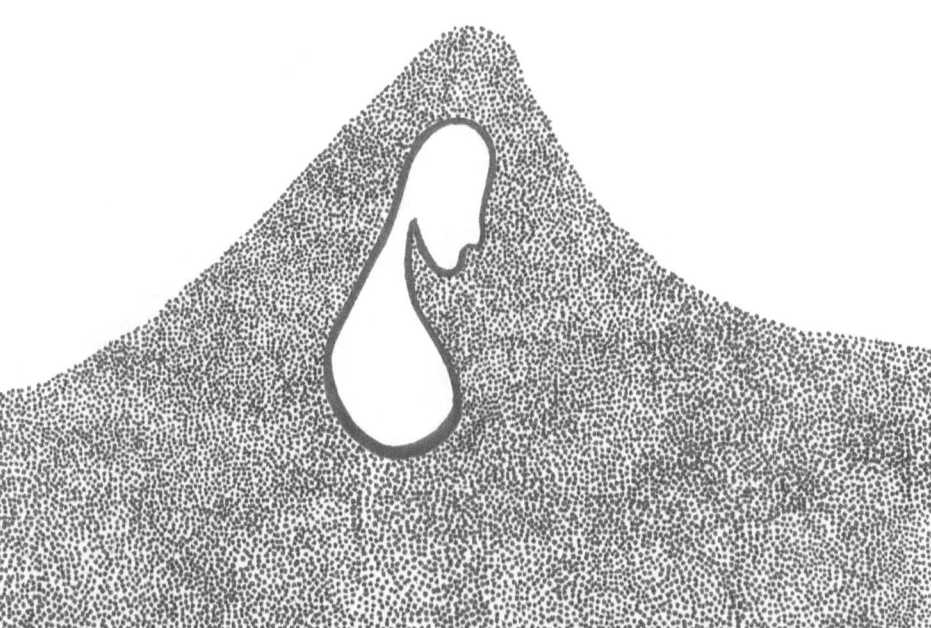

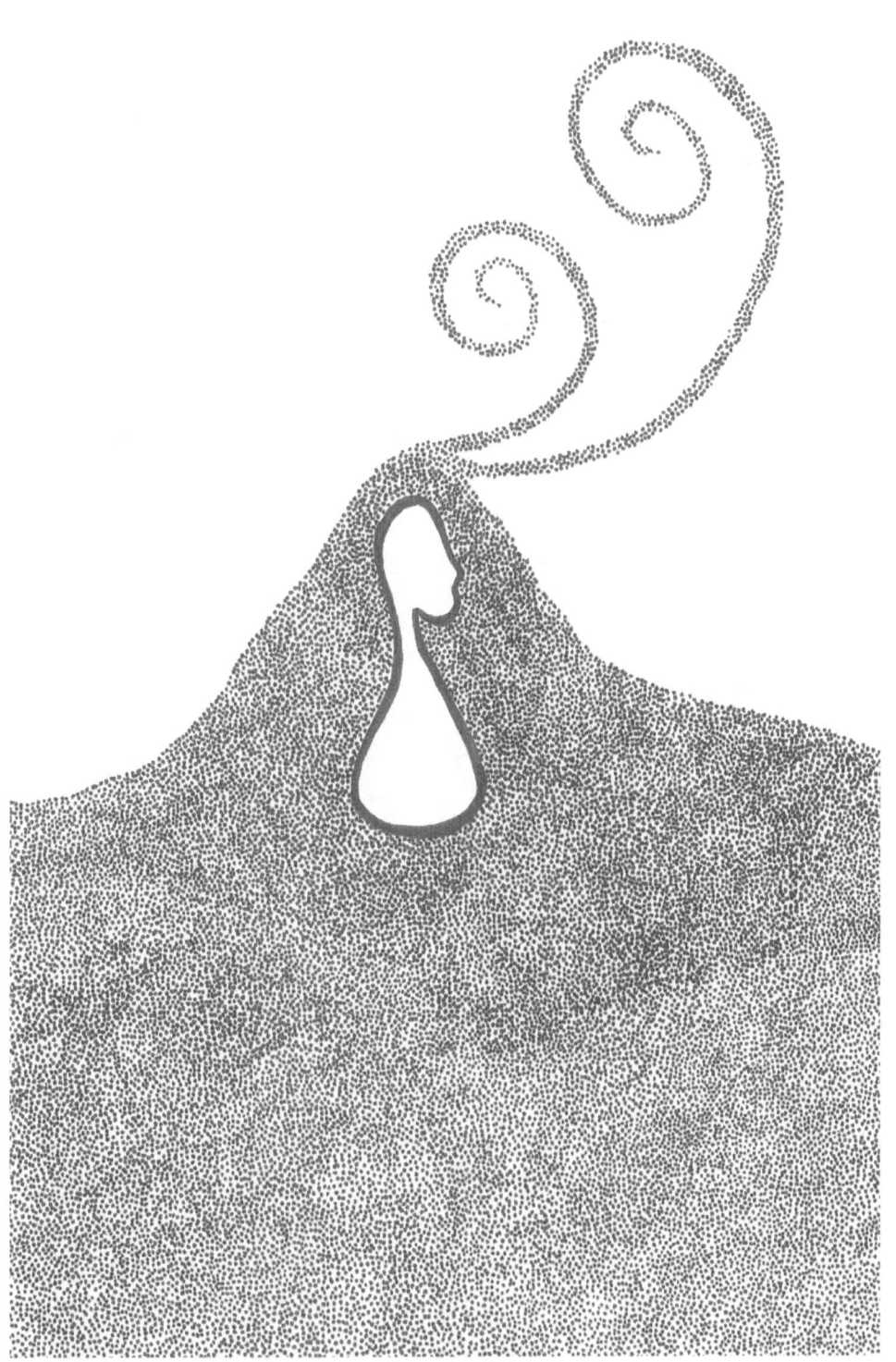

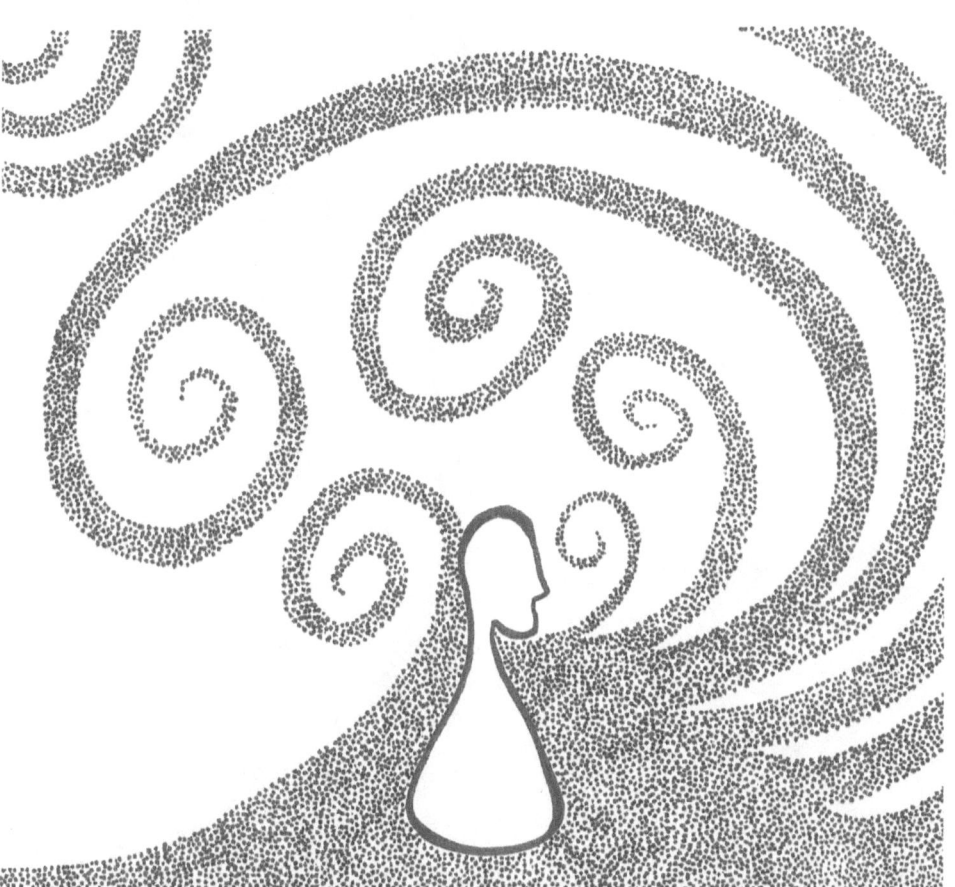

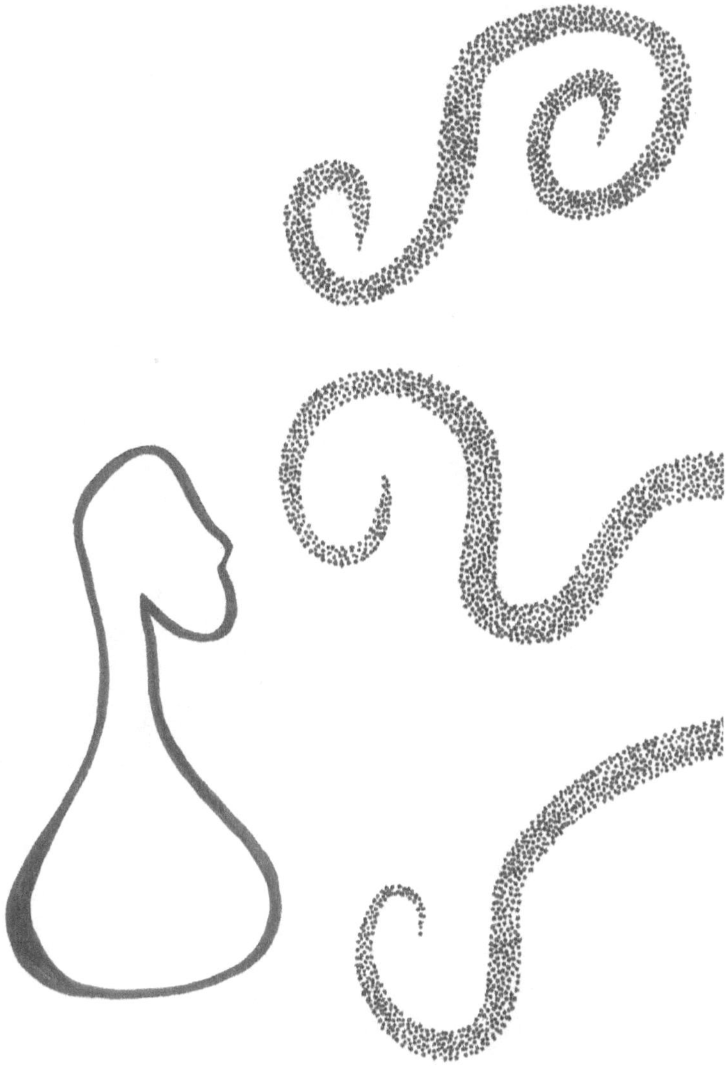

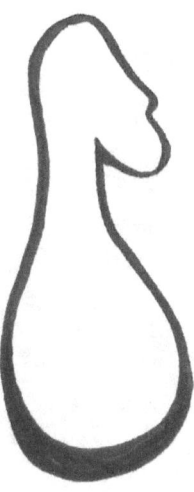

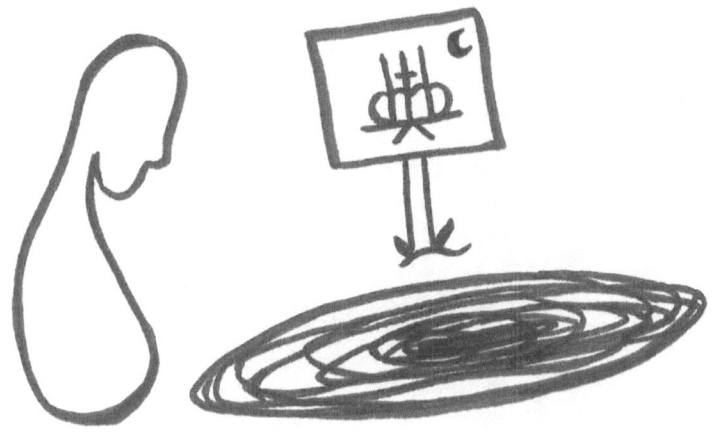

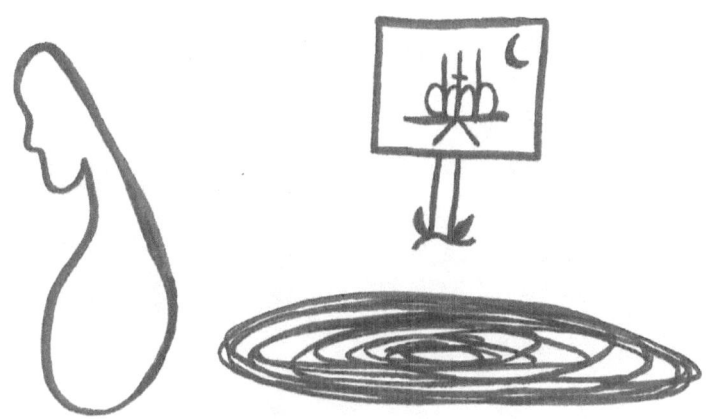

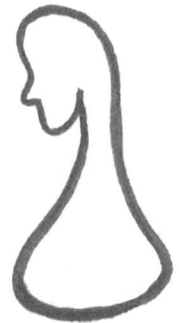
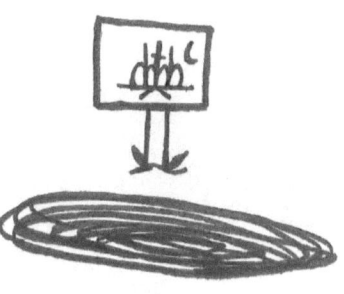

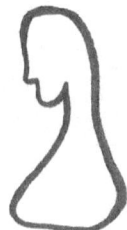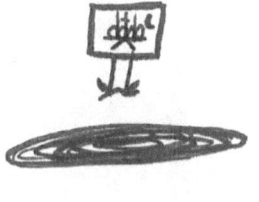

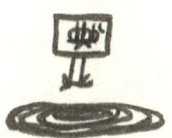
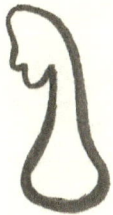

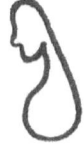